Conceptual
PHYSICS

Third Edition

Concept-Development
Practice Book

Paul G. Hewitt

Scott Foresman
Addison Wesley

Editorial Offices: Menlo Park, California • Glenview, Illinois
Sales Offices: Reading, Massachusetts • Atlanta, Georgia • Glenview, Illinois •
Carrollton, Texas • Menlo Park, California

http://www.sf.aw.com

Contents

Chapter	Practice	Page
1 About Science	1-1	1
2 Linear Motion	2-1	3
	2-2	5
3 Projectile Motion	3-1	7
	3-2	9
4 Newton's First Law of Motion—Inertia	4-1	11
	4-2	13
	4-3	15
5 Newton's Second Law of Motion—Force and Acceleration	5-1	17
	5-2	19
	5-3	21
	5-4	23
	5-5	25
6 Newton's Third Law of Motion—Action and Reaction	6-1	27
7 Momentum	7-1	29
8 Energy	8-1	31
	8-2	33
	8-3	35
9 Circular Motion	9-1	37
	9-2	39
	9-3	41
10 Center of Gravity	10-1	43
11 Rotational Mechanics	11-1	45
	11-2	47
12 Universal Gravitation	12-1	49
13 Gravitational Interactions	13-1	51
	13-2	53
	13-3	55
14 Satellite Motion	14-1	57
15 Special Relativity—Space and Time	15-1	59
16 Special Relativity—Length, Momentum, and Energy	16-1	61
2 - 14 Mechanics Overview	16-1b	62
17 Atomic Nature of Matter	17-1	63
18 Solids	18-1	65
	18-2	67
19 Liquids	19-1	69
	19-2	71

Chapter	Practice	Page
20 Gases	20-1	73
	20-2	75
21 Temperature, Heat, and Expansion	21-1	77
	21-2	79
22 Heat Transfer	22-1	81
23 Change of Phase	23-1	83
	23-2	85
24 Thermodynamics	24-1	87
25 Vibrations and Waves	25-1	89
	25-2	91
	25-3	93
26 Sound	26-1	95
27 Light	27-1	97
	27-2	99
28 Color	28-1	101
29 Reflection and Refraction	29-1	103
	29-2	105
	29-3	107
	29-4	109
30 Lenses	30-1	111
	30-1	113
31 Diffraction and Interference	31-1	115
32 Electrostatics	32-1	117
	32-2	119
33 Electric Fields and Potential	33-1	121
	33-2	123
34 Electric Current	34-1	125
	34-2	127
35 Electric Circuits	35-1	129
	35-2	131
36 Magnetism	36-1	133
37 Electromagnetic Induction	37-1	135
	37-2	137
38 The Atom and the Quantum	38-1	139
39 The Atomic Nucleus and Radioactivity	39-1	141
	39-2	143
40 Nuclear Fission and Fusion	40-1	145

To The Student

We all like to enjoy ourselves. One of the things we enjoy is finding we can do something that we thought we couldn't, like throwing a ball farther than we thought we could, or performing an acrobatic feat we thought only other people could do. It's also fun to get the best from our brains—to discover we can really understand concepts and ideas we thought we couldn't. These practice pages will help you to do that with the basic science—physics.

These practice pages are to teach you—not to test. Use your textbook with these pages, and consult your classmates when you need help. Your teacher will probably not grade these, but will instead base your grade on test scores (that will indirectly relate to how well you get into these practice pages). These pages are to help you get the hang of physics—something you will likely find enjoyable and worthwhile.

To The Teacher

The purpose of these practice pages is to teach—not to test. Students will learn from them and find that learning physics can be an enjoyable activity— especially if the practice pages are non-threatening. We strongly suggest that teachers do not grade these, but rather write comments on them and use them as a basis for class discussions. Ample test material is provided in the test bank supplement.

These are *concept-development* practice pages and are designed for the second stage of the three-stage learning cycle. As such they should not be used before your students have done at least one Exploratory Activity from the Conceptual Physics Laboratory Manual, or before the chapter material has been treated in class.

Some algebra is used in some pages. A more challenging pair of pages (13-3b), for example, algebraically transforms the inverse-square law for gravitation to the inverse-cube law for tidal gravity. For algebraically weak students, this page can be either skipped or assigned with supporting instruction. Some of the pages require simple computation to help the student better learn the concept—for example, what keeps a 100-W bulb lit in terms of the number of swimming pools of water that go over a dam at the power plant (37-2b). These more mathematical exercises overlap the third stage of the learning cycle: Concept Application.

Encourage students to works in pairs or small groups. Assign a page to one of the students, who is to sign "prepared by." The other(s) are to sign "checked by," and after review and rewrite, the teacher approves. This method acquaints your students with the standard practice of science and engineering firms. Good work can be duplicated for class discussion and/or bulletin board posting.

Use and enjoy!

Dedicated to

Clarence Bakken

Howard Brand

Marshall Ellenstein

Acknowledgments

For their insightful contributions to this edition, I am especially grateful to the three high school teachers listed above—to whom this book is dedicated. I am also very grateful to my resourceful assistants, Ken Ford and Charlie Spiegel for their feedback to these practice pages (and every other phase of Conceptual Physics). For valued input that goes back to Practice Pages of previous editions I remain grateful to Judith Christensen, Clint Clausen, Rosemary Davidson, Craig and Lila Dawson, Paul Doherty, Steve Hammack, Lloyd Harrich, Jim Hill, Peter Hopkinson, Meidor Hu, Brad Huff, Dack Lee, Cherie Bibo Lehman, Chelcie and Kathy Liu, Suzanne Lyons, Fred Muller, Pablo Robinson, Peter Saxby, Nate Unterman, Wallace Williamson, and Barbara Wolfe.

For helpful suggestions and feedback to new ideas for this third edition I thank Bob Becker, Jim Court, Charlie Emmert, Art Fortgang, Jerry Hosken, Dack Lee, Tom Maccarone, Carl Rotter, and Kelly Woods.

I am grateful to Meidor Hu for her help in page layout and production.

Name _____ Period _____ Date _____

Making Hypotheses

The word *science* comes from Latin, meaning "to know." The word *hypothesis* comes from Greek, "under an idea." A hypothesis (an educated guess) often leads to new knowledge and may help to establish a theory.

Examples:

1. We see items in a store priced at $2.98, or $3.98, or $4.98 etc. Why not $3, $4, or $5, etc? Make a hypothesis for this by finishing the following:

   Items in a store are usually priced one or two cents lower than the nearest dollar because

   _____

   _____

   _____

   _____

   Suggest a way to test this hypothesis. (Hint: Imagine you own a chain of stores.)

   _____

   _____

   _____

   _____

   Another hypothesis is based on distrust of sales clerks before the use of cash registers. In those days money was handled only by store owners. A customer buying a $5 item would give a $5 bill to the clerk who might "forget" to give it to the store owner at the cashier's window. At $4.98 the customer wants the change (2 cents), and so the clerk must go to the store owner to get it. Thus tradition and a custom started. How could you support the hypothesis that store owners established pricing policies to protect themselves against sales clerks ? (Hint: Imagine you have a librarian friend who has information on F.W. Woolworth.)

   _____

   _____

   _____

Conceptual **PHYSICS**

2. It is well known that things generally expand when heated. An iron plate gets slightly bigger, for example, when put in a hot oven. But what of a hole in the middle of the iron? Will the hole get bigger or smaller when expansion occurs? One friend says the size of the hole will increase, and another says it will decrease.

> I CUT A DISK FROM THIS IRON PLATE. WHEN I HEAT THE PLATE, WILL THE HOLE GET BIGGER, OR SMALLER?

a. What is your hypothesis about hole size, and if you are wrong, is there a test for finding out?

_____

_____

_____

_____

> WHAT HAPPENS IF HE PLUGS THE DISK BACK INTO THE HOLE BEFORE HEATING EVERYTHING?

b. here are often several ways to test a hypothesis. For example, you can perform a physical experiment and witness the results yourself, or you can use the library to find the reported results of other investigators. Which of these two methods do you favor, and why?

_____

_____

3. Before the time of the printing press, books were hand-copied by scribes, many of whom were monks in monasteries. There is the story of the scribe who was frustrated to find a smudge on an important page he was copying. The smudge blotted out part of the sentence that reported the number of teeth in the head of a donkey. The scribe was very upset and didn't know what to do. He consulted with other scribes to see if any of their books stated the number of teeth in the head of a donkey. After many hours of fruitless searching through the library, it was agreed that the best thing to do was to send a messenger by donkey to the next monastery and continue the search there. What would be your advice?

_____

_____

_____

MAKING DISTINCTIONS

Many people don't seem to see the difference between a thing and the *abuse* of the thing. For example, a city council that bans skateboards may not distinguish between skateboarding and reckless skateboarding. A person who advocates that technology be banned may not distinguish between technology and the abuses of technology. There is a difference between a thing and the abuse of the thing. On a separate sheet of paper, list examples you can think of — then discuss your list and those of others with classmates.

Conceptual **PHYSICS**

Non-Accelerated Motion

1. The sketch shows a ball rolling at constant velocity along a level floor. The ball rolls from the first position shown to the second in 1 second. The two positons are 1 meter apart. Sketch the ball at successive 1-second intervals all the way to the wall (neglect resistance).

a. Did you draw successive ball positions evenly spaced, farther apart, or closer together? Why?

_____

b. The ball reaches the wall with a speed of _____ m/s and takes a time of _____ seconds.

2. Table I shows data of sprinting speeds of some animals. Make whatever computations are necessary to complete the table.

Table I

ANIMAL	DISTANCE	TIME	SPEED
CHEETAH	75 m	3 s	25 m/s
GREYHOUND	160 m	10 s	
GAZELLE	1 km		100 km/h
TURTLE		30 s	1 cm/s

Accelerated Motion

3. An object starting from rest gains a speed $v = at$ when it undergoes uniform acceleration. The distance it covers is $d = 1/2\ at^2$. Uniform acceleration occurs for a ball rolling down an inclined plane. The plane below is tilted so a ball picks up a speed of 2 m/s each second; then its acceleration $a = 2$ m/s^2. The positions of the ball are shown for 1-second intervals. Complete the six blank spaces for distance covered, and the four blank spaces for speeds.

a. Do you see that the total distance from the starting point increases as the square of the time? This was discovered by Galileo. If the incline were to continue, predict the ball's distance from the starting point for the next 3 seconds.

_____

b. Note the increase of distance between ball positions with time. Do you see an odd-integer pattern (also discovered by Galileo) for this increase? If the incline were to continue, predict the successive distances between ball positions for the next 3 seconds.

_____

Now you're ready for "Merrily We Roll Along!" in the lab manual!

conceptual PHYSICS

Free Fall

4. A rock dropped from the top of a cliff picks up speed as it falls. Pretend that a speedometer and odometer are attached to the rock to show readings of speed and distance at 1-second intervals. Both speed and distance are zero at time = zero (see sketch). Note that after falling 1 second the speed reading is 10 m/s and the distance fallen is 5 m. The readings for succeeding seconds of fall are not shown and are left for you to complete. So draw the position of the speedometer pointer and write in the correct odometer reading for each time. Use $g = 10$ m/s² and neglect air resistance.

RELATIONSHIPS TO USE
Instantaneous speed of fall from rest:
$$v = gt$$
Distance fallen from rest:
$$d = \frac{1}{2}gt^2$$

a. The speedometer reading increases by the same amount, _____ m/s, each second. This increase in speed per second is called _____.

b. The distance fallen increases as the square of the _____.

c. If it takes 7 seconds to reach the ground, then its speed at impact is _____ m/s, the total distance fallen is _____ m, and its acceleration of fall just before impact is _____ m/s².

Conceptual PHYSICS

Projectile Motion

1. Above left: Use the scale 1 cm: 5 m and draw the positions of the dropped ball at 1-second intervals. Neglect air drag and assume $g = 10$ m/s². Estimate the number of seconds the ball is in the air.

    _____ seconds.

2. Above right: The four positions of the thrown ball with *no gravity* are at 1-second intervals. At 1 cm: 5 m, carefully draw the positions of the ball *with* gravity. Neglect air drag and assume $g = 10$ m/s². Connect your positions with a smooth curve to show the path of the ball. How is the motion in the vertical direction affected by motion in the horizontal direction?

_____

Conceptual **PHYSICS**

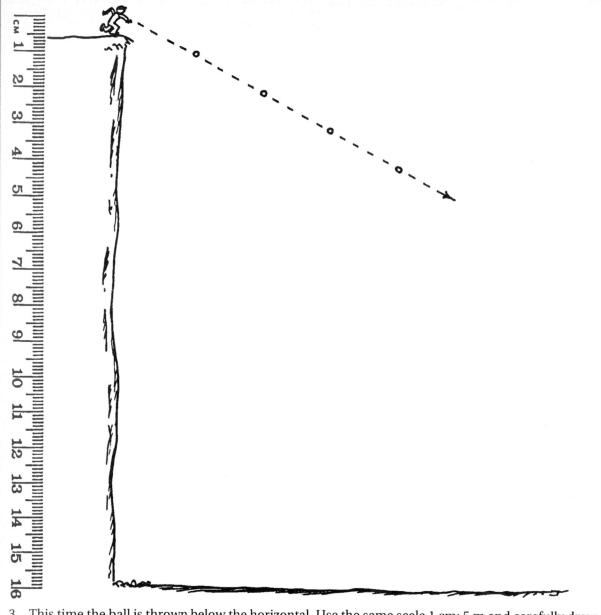

3. This time the ball is thrown below the horizontal. Use the same scale 1 cm: 5 m and carefully draw the positions of the ball as it falls beneath the dashed line. Connect your positions with a smooth curve. Estimate the number of seconds the ball remains in the air._____ s

4. Suppose that you are an accident investigator and you are asked to figure whether or not the car was speeding before it crashed through the rail of the bridge and into the mudbank as shown. The speed limit on the bridge is 55 mph = 24 m/s. What is your conclusion?

_____

_____

_____

Vectors

Use the parallelogram rule to carefully construct the resultants for the eight pairs of vectors.

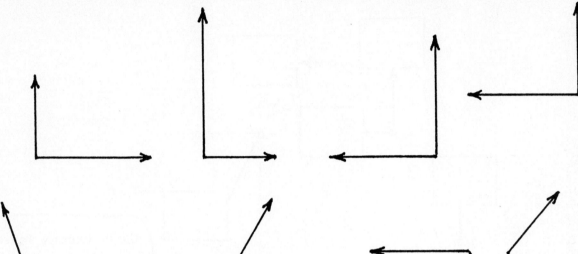

Carefully construct the vertical and horizontal components of the eight vectors.

I was only a scalar until you came along and gave me direction! ≥sigh≥

Conceptual PHYSICS

Tossed Ball

A ball tossed upward has initial velocity components 30 m/s vertical, and 5 m/s horizontal. The position of the ball is shown at 1-second intervals. Air resistance is negligible, and $g = 10$ m/s^2. Fill in the boxes, writing in the values of velocity *components* ascending, and your calculated *resultant velocities* descending.

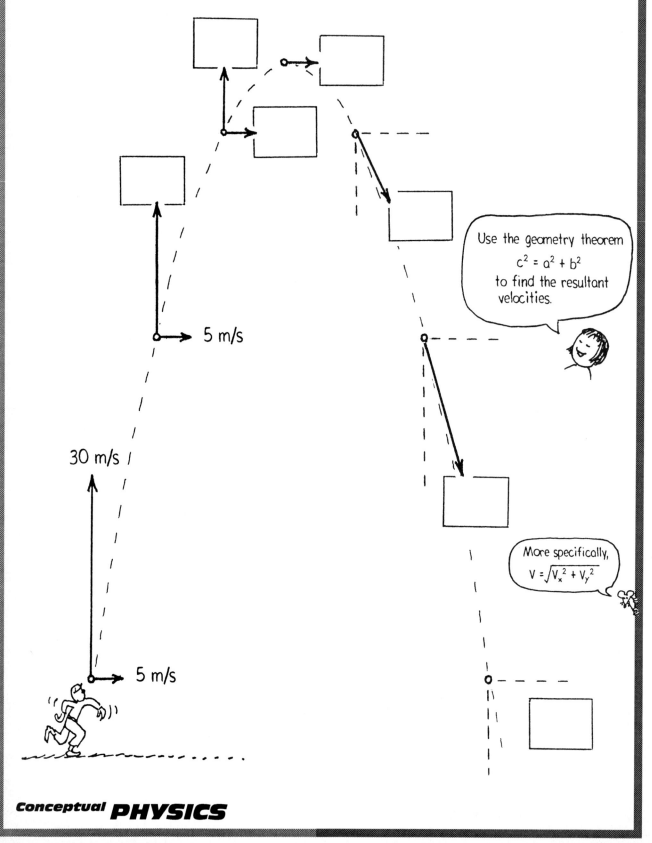

5 m/s

30 m/s

5 m/s

Use the geometry theorem
$$c^2 = a^2 + b^2$$
to find the resultant velocities.

More specifically,
$$V = \sqrt{V_x^2 + V_y^2}$$

Conceptual **PHYSICS**

**Concept-Development
Practice Page**   **4-1**

1. (*Circle the correct answer.*) An astronaut in outer space away from gravitational or frictional forces throws a rock. The rock will

    (gradually slow to a stop)

    (continue moving in a straight line at constant speed)

The rock's tendency to do this is called

    (inertia)   (weight)   (acceleration)

2.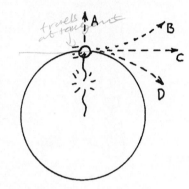

The sketch shows a top view of a rock being whirled at the end of a string (clockwise). If the string breaks, the path of the rock is

    (A) (B) (C) (D)

3. Suppose you are standing in the aisle of a bus that travels along a straight road at 100 km/h, and you hold a pencil still above your head. Then relative to the bus, the velocity of the pencil is 0 km/h, and relative to the road, the pencil has a horizontal velocity of

    (less than 100 km/h)   100 km/h   (more than 100 km/h)

Suppose you release the pencil. While it is dropping, and relative to the road, the pencil still has a horizontal velocity of

    (less than 100 km/h)   (100 km/h) (more than 100 km/h)

This means that the pencil will strike the floor at a place directly

    (behind you) (at your feet below your hand) in front of you)

Relative to you, the way the pencil drops

    (is the same as if the bus were at rest)

    (depends on the velocity of the bus)

How does this example illustrate the law of inertia?

travelling at a straight line in horizontal direction (no force)
and down in vertical.
    does not travel unless there's a force (in straight line

Conceptual **PHYSICS**

     Chapter 4   Newton's First Law of Motion —Inertia   **11**

4. Use the words *mass*, *weight*, and *volume*, to complete the table.

The force due to gravity on an object	weight
The quantity of matter in an object	mass
The amount of space an object occupies	volume

5. Different masses are hung on a spring scale calibrated in newtons.

The force exerted by gravity on 1 kg = 9.8 N.

The force exerted by gravity on 5 kg = __49__ N.

The force exerted by gravity on __10__ kg = 98 N.

Make up your own mass and show the corresponding weight:

The force exerted by gravity on __7__ kg = __68.6__ N.

6. By whatever means (spring scales, measuring balance, etc.), find the mass of your physics book. Then complete Table I.

OBJECT	MASS	WEIGHT
MELON	1 kg	9.8N
APPLE	0.1kg	1 N
PHYSICS BOOK	0.5kg	4.9N
UNCLE HARRY	90 kg	882N

Table I

7. Why isn't the girl hurt when the nail is driven into the block of wood?

only lifting nail, little force won't move the wood
_____

Would this be more dangerous or less dangerous if the block were less massive _____? Explain.

_____

_____

_____

CAUTION: Safety dictates you not try this experiment yourself.

Conceptual **PHYSICS**

Concept-Development Practice Page   **4-2**

Statics

1. Little Nellie Newton wishes to be a gymnast and hangs from a variety of positions as shown. Since she is not accelerating, the net force on her is zero. This means the upward pull of the rope(s) equals the downward pull of gravity. She weighs 300 N. Show the scale reading for each case.

2. When Burl the painter stands in the exact middle of his staging, the left scale reads 500 N. Fill in the reading on the right scale. The total weight of Burl and staging must be

_____ N.

3. Burl stands farther from the left. Fill in the reading on the right scale.

4. In a silly mood, Burl dangles from the right end. Fill in the reading on the right scale.

Conceptual PHYSICS

    Chapter 4   Newton's First Law of Motion —Inertia   **13**

Vectors and Equilibrium

The rock hangs at rest from a single string. Only two forces act on it, the upward tension **T** of the string, and the downward pull of gravity **W**. The forces are equal in magnitude and opposite in direction.

Net force on the rock is (zero) (greater than zero).

Here the rock is suspended by 2 strings. Tension in each string acts in a direction along the string. We'll show tension of the left string by vector **A**, and tension of the right string by vector **B**. The resultant of **A** and **B** is found by the ***parallelogram rule***, and is shown by the dashed vector. Note it has the same magnitude as **W**, so the net force on the rock is

(zero) (greater than zero).

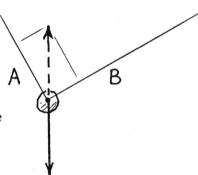

Consider strings at unequal angles. The resultant **A** + **B** is still equal and opposite to **W**, and is shown by the dashed vector. Construct the appropriate parallelogram to produce this resultant. Show the relative magnitudes of **A** and **B**.

Tension in **A** is (less than) (equal to) (greater than) tension in **B**.

Repeat the procedure for the arrangement below.

Here tension is greater in _____.

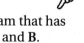

Construct vectors **A** and **B** for the cases below. First draw a vector **W**, then the parallelogram that has equal and opposite vector **A** + **B** as the diagonal. Then find approximate magnitudes of **A** and **B**.

Conceptual **PHYSICS**

Force and Velocity Vectors

1. Draw sample vectors to represent the force of gravity on the ball in the positions shown above (after it leaves the thrower's hand). Neglect air drag.

2. Draw sample bold vectors to represent the velocity of the ball in the positions shown above. With lighter vectors, show the horizontal and vertical components of velocity for each position.

3. (a) Which velocity component in the previous question remains constant ? Why?

_____

(b) Which velocity component changes along the path? Why?

_____

4. It is important to distinguish between force and velocity vectors. Force vectors combine with other force vectors, and velocity vectors combine with other velocity vectors. Do velocity vectors combine with force vectors? _____

5. All forces on the bowling ball, weight down and support of alley up, are shown by vectors at its center before it strikes the pin (*a*). Draw vectors of all the forces that act on the ball (*b*) when it strikes the pin, and (*c*) after it strikes the pin.

(a)   (b)   (c)

Conceptual **PHYSICS**

thanx to Howard Brand

    Chapter 4   Newton's First Law of Motion —Inertia

Net Force

Fill in the magnitudes of net force for each case.

$F_{net} = \underline{\hspace{1cm}}$

$F_{net} = \underline{\hspace{1cm}}$

$F_{net} = \underline{\hspace{1cm}}$

$F_{net} = \underline{\hspace{1cm}}$

$F_{net} = \underline{\hspace{1cm}}$

$F_{net} = \underline{\hspace{1cm}}$

$F_{net} = \underline{\hspace{1cm}}$

$F_{net} = \underline{\hspace{1cm}}$

$F_{net} = \underline{\hspace{1cm}}$

$F_{net} = \underline{\hspace{1cm}}$

Force and Acceleration

1. Skelly the skater, total mass 25 kg, is propelled by rocket power.

   a. Complete Table I
      (neglect resistance)

   TABLE I

FORCE	ACCELERATION
100 N	
200 N	
	10 m/s²

   b. Complete Table II for a
      constant 50-N resistance.

   TABLE II

FORCE	ACCELERATION
50 N	0 m/s²
100 N	
200 N	

2. Block A on a horizontal friction-free table is accelerated by a force from
   a string attached to Block B. B falls vertically and drags A horizontally.
   Both blocks have the same mass m. (Neglect the string's mass.)

   (Circle the correct answers)

   a. The *mass* of the system [A + B] is (m) (2 m).

   b. The *force* that accelerates [A + B] is the weight of (A) (B) (A + B).

   c. The weight of B is (mg/2) (mg) (2 mg).

   d. Acceleration of [A + B] is (less than g) (g) (more than g).

   e. Use $a =$ to show the acceleration of [A + B] as a fraction of g._____

If B were allowed to fall by itself, not dragging A,
then wouldn't its acceleration be g?

Yes, because the force that accelerates
it would only be acting on its own
mass — not twice the mass!

To better understand this,
consider 3 and 4 on the
other side!

Conceptual PHYSICS

    Chapter 5   Newton's Second Law of Motion—Force and Acceleration

Force and Acceleration continued

3. Suppose A is still a 1-kg block, but B is a low-mass feather (or a coin).

   a. Compared to the acceleration of the system in 2, previous page,
      the acceleration of [A + B] here is (less) (more)
      and is (close to zero) (close to *g*).

   b. In this case the acceleration of B is
      (practically that of free fall) (constrained).

4. Suppose A is a feather or coin, and B has a mass of 1 kg.

   a. The acceleration of [A + B] here is
      (close to zero) (close to *g*).

   b. In this case the acceleration of B is
      (practically that of free fall) (constrained).

5. Summarizing 2, 3, and 4, where the weight of one object causes the acceleration of two objects,
   we see the range of possible accelerations is

   (between zero and *g*) (between zero and infinity) (between *g* and infinity).

6. A ball rolls down a uniform-slope ramp.

   a. Acceleration is (decreasing) (constant) (increasing).

   b. If the ramp were steeper, acceleration would be
      (more) (the same) (less).

   c. When the ball reaches the bottom and rolls along the smooth level surface it
      (continues to accelerate) (does not accelerate).

> Now you're ready for the labs " Constant Force and Changing Mass "
> and " Constant Mass and Changing Force "!

Conceptual **PHYSICS**

Name _____ Period _____ Date _____

Equilibrium on an Inclined Plane

1. The block is at rest on a horizontal surface. The normal support force **n** is equal and opposite to weight **W**.

    a. There is (friction) (no friction) because the block has no tendency to slide.

2. At rest on the incline, friction acts. Note [right] the resultant **f + n** [dashed vector] is equal and opposite to **W**.

    a. Here we see that the size of **n** is (less than) (equal to) (greater than) the size of **W**.

3. You draw the resultant **f + n** for the block at rest on the steeper incline.

    a. The resultant magnitude of **f + n** is (less than) (equal to) (greater than) the magnitude of **W**.

    b. As the angle of the incline increases, the magnitude of vector **n** (decreases) (stays the same) (increases).

Can you also see that n + W = -f? And f + W = -n? Vectors make sense!

4. The block remains at rest on the still steeper incline. You draw vectors for equilibrium.

    a. How does the resultant **f + n** compare to **W**?

    b. Suppose the angle is increased and the block slides down the incline at constant velocity. Then the net force on the block is (zero) (greater than zero). If the angle is increased even further, then acceleration (occurs) (doesn't occur).

5. Further steepness of the incline means (less) (more) acceleration down the plane. When the incline is vertical, acceleration is (less than *g*) (*g*) (more than *g*).

Conceptual PHYSICS

Force-Vector Diagrams

In each case, a rock is acted on by one or more forces. Draw an accurate vector diagram showing all forces acting on the rock, and no other forces. Use a ruler, and do it in pencil so you can correct mistakes. The first two are done as examples. Show by the parallelogram rule in 2 that the vector sum of **A** + **B** is equal and opposite to **W** (that is, **A** + **B** = -**W**). Do the same for 3 and 4. Draw and label vectors for the weight and normal forces in 5 to 10, and for the appropriate forces in 11 and 12.

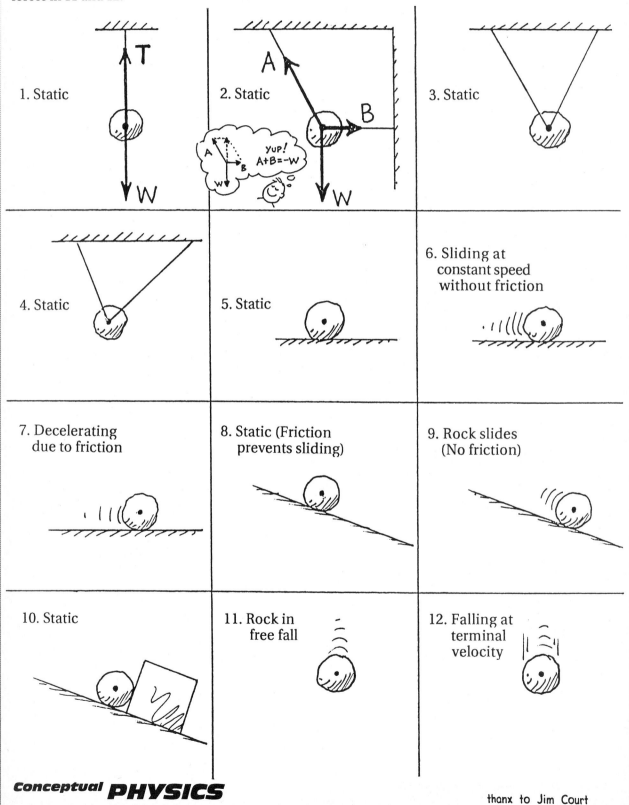

1. Static

2. Static

3. Static

4. Static

5. Static

6. Sliding at constant speed without friction

7. Decelerating due to friction

8. Static (Friction prevents sliding)

9. Rock slides (No friction)

10. Static

11. Rock in free fall

12. Falling at terminal velocity

Conceptual *PHYSICS*

thanx to Jim Court

**Concept-Development
Practice Page**

5-5

Sailboats

(Do not attempt this until you have studied Appendix D!)

1. The sketch shows a top view of a small railroad car pulled by a rope. The force *F* that the rope exerts on the car has one component along the track, and another component perpendicular to the track.

   a. Draw these components on the sketch. Which component is larger?

      _____

   b. Which component produces acceleration?

      _____

   c. What would be the effect of pulling on the rope if it were perpendicular to the track?

      _____

2. The sketches below represent simplified top views of sailboats in a cross-wind direction. The impact of the wind produces a FORCE vector on each as shown.
(We do NOT consider *velocity* vectors here!)

   a. Why is the position of the sail above useless for propelling the boat along its forward direction? (Relate this to Question 1c. above. Where the train is constrained by tracks to move in one direction, the boat is similarly constrained to move along one direction by its deep vertical fin — the *keel.*)

      _____

      _____

   b. Sketch the component of force parallel to the direction of the boat's motion (along its keel), and the component perpendicular to its motion. Will the boat move in a forward direction? (Relate this to Question 1b. above.)

      _____

      _____

Conceptual **PHYSICS**

   Chapter 5   Newton's Second Law of Motion—Force and Acceleration

3. The boat to the right is oriented at an angle into the wind. Draw the force vector and its forward and perpendicular components.

   a. Will the boat move in a forward direction and tack into the wind? Why or why not?

   _____

   _____

4. The sketch below is a top view of five identical sailboats. Where they exist, draw force vectors to represent wind impact on the sails. Then draw components parallel and perpendicular to the keels of each boat.

   a. Which boat will sail the fastest in a forward direction?

   _____

   b. Which will respond least to the wind?

   _____

   c. Which will move in a backward direction?

   _____

   d. Which will experience less and less wind impact with increasing speed?

   _____

Conceptual **PHYSICS**

Work and Energy

1. How much work (energy) is needed to lift an object that weighs 200 N to a height of 4 m?

   _____

2. How much power is needed to lift the 200-N object to a height of 4 m in 4 s?

   _____

3. What is the power output of an engine that does 60 000 J of work in 10 s?

   _____

4. The block of ice weighs 500 newtons.

   a. What is the mechanical advantage of the incline?

   _____

   b. How much force is needed to push it
      up the incline (neglect friction)?

   _____

5. All the ramps are 5 m high. We know that the KE of the block at the bottom of the ramp will be equal to the loss of PE (conservation of energy). Find the speed of the block at ground level in each case. [Hint: Do you recall from earlier chapters how long it takes something to fall a vertical distance of 5 m from a positon of rest (assume $g = 10$ m/s²)? And how much speed a falling object acquires in this time? This gives you the answer to Case 1. Discuss with your classmates how energy conservation gives you the answers to Cases 2 and 3.]

Case 1: Speed = _____ m/s   Case 2: Speed = _____ m/s   Case 3: Speed = _____ m/s.

Conceptual **PHYSICS**

6. Which block gets to the bottom of the incline first? Assume no friction. (Be careful!) Explain your answer.

_____

_____

_____

7. The KE and PE of a block freely sliding down a ramp are shown in only one place in the sketch. Fill in the missing values.

PE = _____
KE = 0

PE = 50 J
KE = _____

PE = _____
KE = 50 J

PE = 0
KE = 75 J

8. A big metal bead slides due to gravity along an upright friction-free wire. It starts from rest at the top of the wire as shown in the sketch. How fast is it traveling as it passes

Point B?_____

Point D?_____

Point E?_____

At what point does it have the

maximum speed?_____

9. Rows of wind-powered generators are used in various windy locations to generate electric power. Does the power generated affect the speed of the wind? Would locations behind the 'windmills' be windier if they weren't there? Discuss this in terms of energy conservation with your classmates.

_____

_____

_____

_____

Momentum and Energy

$t = 0$ s $v =$ _____
        momentum = _____

$t = 1$ s $v =$ _____
        momentum = _____

$t = 2$ s $v =$ _____
        momentum = _____

$t = 3$ s $v =$ _____
        momentum = _____

$t = 5$ s $v =$ _____
        momentum = _____

Bronco Brown wants to put $Ft = \Delta mv$ to the test and try bungee jumping. Bronco leaps from a high cliff and experiences free fall for 3 seconds. Then the bungee cord begins to stretch, reducing his speed to zero in 2 seconds. Fortunately, the cord stretches to its maximum length just short of the ground below.

Fill in the blanks. Bronco's mass is 100 kg. Acceleration of free fall is 10 m/s².

Express values in SI units (*distance* in m, *velocity* in m/s, *momentum* in kg-m/s, *impulse* in N-s, and *deceleration* in m/s²).

The 3-s free-fall distance of Bronco just before the bungee cord begins to stretch

= _____

Δmv during the 3-s interval of free fall

= _____

Δmv during the 2-s interval of slowing down

= _____

Impulse during the 2-s interval of slowing down

= _____

Average force exerted by the cord during the 2-s interval of slowing down

= _____

How about *work* and *energy*? How much KE does Bonco have 3 s after his jump?

_____

How much does gravitational PE decrease during this 3 s? _____

What two kinds of PE are changing during the slowing-down interval?

_____

Conceptual **PHYSICS**

Energy and Momentum

A Honda Civic and a Lincoln Town Car are initially at rest on a horizontal parking lot at the edge of a steep cliff. For simplicity, we assume that the Town Car has twice as much mass as the Civic. Equal constant forces are applied to each car and they accelerate across equal distances (we ignore the effects of friction). When they reach the far end of the lot the force is suddenly removed, whereupon they sail through the air and crash to the ground below. (The cars are beat up to begin with, and this is a scientific experiment!)

> Let equations guide your thinking!

1. Which car has the greater acceleration ? _____

2. Which car spends more time along the surface of the lot? _____

3. Which car is moving faster when it reaches the edge of the cliff? _____

4. Which car has the larger impulse imparted to it by the applied force? Defend your answer.

_____

5. Which car has the greater momentum at the edge of the cliff? Defend your answer.

_____

> Impulse $= \Delta$ momentum
> $Ft = \Delta mv$

> Work $= Fd = \Delta KE = \Delta \frac{1}{2}mv^2$

6. Which car has the greater work done on it by the applied force?
   Defend your answer in terms of the distance traveled.

_____

7. Which car has the greater kinetic energy at the edge of the cliff?
   Does your answer follow from your explanation of 6?
   Does it contradict your answer to 4? Why or why not?

> Making the distinction between momentum and kinetic energy is high-level physics!

_____

8. Which car spends more time in the air, from the edge of the cliff to the ground below? _____

9. Which car lands farthest horizontally from the edge of the cliff onto the ground below? _____

10. Challenge: Suppose the slower car crashes a horizontal distance of 10 m from the ledge. Then at what horizontal distance does the faster car hit?

_____

***Conceptual* PHYSICS**

Concept-Development Practice Page   **9-1**

Circular Motion

1. Most energy of train systems is used in starting and stopping. The *rotating train platform* design saves energy, for people can board or leave a train while the train is still moving. Study the sketch and convince yourself that this is true. The small circular platform in the middle is stationary, and is connected to a stationary stairway.

     a. If there is to be no relative motion between the train and the edge of the platform, how fast must the train move compared to the rim speed of the rotating platform?

     _____

     b. Why is the stairway located at the center of the platform?

     _____

2. The design below shows a train that makes round trips from Station A to Station B in a continuous loop.

     a. How is the size of the round platform and train speed related to the amount of time that passengers have for boarding?

     _____

     _____

     b. Why would this rotating platform be impractical for high-speed trains?

     _____

Conceptual PHYSICS

3. Here are some people standing on a giant rotating platform in a fun house. In the view shown, the platform is not rotating and the people stand at rest.

When the platform rotates, the person in the middle stands as before. The person at the edge must lean inward as shown. Make a sketch of the missing people to show how they must lean in comparison.

4. The sketch at the left shows a stationary container of water and some floating toy ducks. The sketch at the right shows the same container rotating about a central axis at constant speed. Note the curved surface of the water. The duck in the center floats as before. Make a sketch to show the orientation of the other two ducks with respect to the water surface.

5. Consider an automobile tire half filled with water. In the cross-sectional views below the left-hand sketch shows the water surface when the tire is not rotating. The right-hand sketch shows the water surface when the tire and water rotate about its central axis.

Now suppose the tire is rotating about the same axis while orbiting in outer space. Draw the shape of the water surface in the cross-sectional view below.

In your mind, scale up the rotating tire model to a rotating space habitat orbiting in space. If the space habitat were half filled with water, could inhabitants float on the surface as they do here on earth? Discuss this with your classmates.

Conceptual **PHYSICS**

Concept-Development Practice Page

9-2

Acceleration and Circular Motion

Newton's 2nd law, $a = F/m$, tells us that net force and its corresponding acceleration are always in the same direction. (Both force and acceleration are vector quantities). But force and acceleration are not always in the direction of velocity (another vector).

1. You're in a car at a traffic light. The light turns green and the driver "steps on the gas."

    a. Your body lurches (forward) (not at all) (backward).

    b. The car accelerates (forward) (not at all) (backward).

    c. The force on the car acts (forward) (not at all) (backward).

       The sketch shows the top view of the car. Note the directions of the velocity and acceleration vectors.

2. You're driving along and approach a stop sign. The driver steps on the brakes.

    a. Your body lurches (forward) (not at all) (backward).

    b. The car accelerates (forward) (not at all) (backward).

    c. The force on the car acts (forward) (not at all) (backward).

       The sketch shows the top view of the car. Draw vectors for velocity and acceleration.

3. You continue driving, and round a sharp curve to the left at constant speed.

    a. Your body leans (inward) (not at all) (outward).

    b. The direction of the car's acceleration is (inward) (not at all) (outward).

    c. The force on the car acts (inward) (not at all) (outward).

       Draw vectors for velocity and acceleration of the car.

4. In general, the directions of lurch and acceleration, and therefore the directions of lurch and force, are (the same) (not related) (opposite).

5. The whirling stone's direction of motion keeps changing.

    a. If it moves faster, its direction changes (faster) (slower).

    b. This indicates that as speed increases, acceleration (increases) (decreases) (stays the same).

6. Consider whirling the stone on a shorter string—that is, of smaller radius.

    a. For a given speed, the rate that the stone changes direction is (less) (more) (the same).

    b. This indicates that as the radius decreases, acceleration (increases) (decreases) (stays the same).

Conceptual PHYSICS

Centripetal Force

1. A rock tied to a post moves in a circle at constant speed on a frictionless horizontal surface. All the forces acting on the rock are shown: Tension T, support force **n** by the table, and the force due to gravity **W**.

   a. The vector responsible for circular motion is _____.

   b. The net force on the rock is _____.

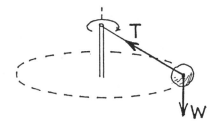

2. In this case the rock is tied to a string and swings in a circular path as shown. It is not resting on a surface. No friction. Use the parallelogram rule and find the resultant of vectors T and W.

   a. What is the direction of the resultant of T and W? _____

   b. Does this resultant lie in the plane of the circular path? _____

   c. Is this resultant also the horizontal component of T? _____

   d. Is the resultant T + W (or the horizontal component of T) a centripetal force? _____

3. In the case shown at the right, the rock rides on a horizontal disk that rotates at constant speed about its vertical axis (dotted line). Friction prevents the rock from sliding.

   a. Draw and label vectors for all forces that act on the rock.

   b. Which force is centripetal? _____

   c. Which force provides the net force? _____

   d. Why do we *not* say the net force is zero? _____

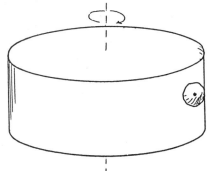

4. Now the rock is held in place by friction against the inside wall of the rotating drum. Draw and label vectors for all forces that act on the rock.

   a. Which force is centripetal? _____

   b. Which force provides the net force? _____

5. More challenging: This time the rock rests against the frictionless inside wall of a cone. It moves with the cone, which rotates about its vertical axis (dotted line). The rock does not slide up or down in the cone as it rotates. Draw and label vectors for all forces that act on the rock.

   Should the resultant force lie in the plane of the circular path? _____

   Why? _____

Note the size of **n** > **W** when **n** contributes to centripetal force!

Conceptual **PHYSICS**

thanx to Jim Court

Concept-Development Practice Page | **9-3**

Simulated Gravity and Frames of Reference

Susie Spacewalker and Bob Biker are in outer space. Bob experiences earth-normal gravity in a rotating habitat, where centripetal force on his feet provides a normal support force that feels like weight. Suzie hovers outside in a weightless condition, motionless relative to the stars and the center of mass of the habitat.

Suzie   Bob

1. Suzie sees Bob rotating clockwise in a circular path at a linear speed of 30 km/h. Suzie and Bob are facing each other, and from Bob's point of view, he is a rest and he sees Suzie moving

   (clockwise) (counter clockwise).

Bob at rest on the floor
Suzie hovering in space

2. The rotating habitat seems like home to Bob—until he rides his bicycle. When he rides in the opposite direction as the habitat rotates, Suzie sees him moving (faster) (slower).

Bob rides counter-clockwise

3. As Bob's bicycle speedometer reading increases, his rotational speed

   (decreases) (remains unchanged) (increases)   and the normal force that feels like weight

   (decreases) (remains unchanged) (increases).   So friction between the tires and the floor

   (decreases) (remains unchanged) (increases).

4. When Bob nevertheless gets his speed up to 30 km/h, as read on his bicycle speedometer, Suzie sees him

   (moving at 30 km/h) (motionless) (moving at 60 km/h)

Conceptual PHYSICS

thanx to Bob Becker

Bob rides at 30 km/h with respect to the floor

5. Bounding off the floor a bit while riding at 30 km/h, and neglecting wind effects, Bob

   (drifts toward the ceiling as the floor whizzes by at 30 km/h)
   (falls as he would on earth)
   (slams onto the floor with increased force).

   and he finds himself

   (in the same frame of reference as Suzie)
   (as if he rode at 30 km/h on the earth's surface)
   (pressed harder against the bicycle seat).

6. Bob manuevers back to his initial condition, whirling at rest with the habitat, standing beside his bicycle. But not for long. Urged by Suzie, he rides in the opposite direction, clockwise with the rotation of the habitat.

   Now Suzie sees him moving (faster) (slower).

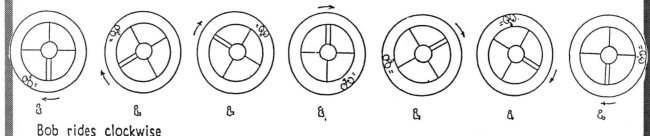

Bob rides clockwise

7. As Bob gains speed, the normal support force that feels like weight

   (decreases) (remains unchanged) (increases).

8. When Bob's speedometer reading gets up to 30 km/h, Suzie sees him moving

   (30 km/h) (not at all) (60 km/h)

   and Bob finds himself

   (weightless like Suzie)
   (just as if he rode at 30 km/h on the earth's surface)
   (pressed harder against the bicycle seat).

Next, Bob goes bowling. You decide whether the game depends on which direction the ball is rolled!

Conceptual **PHYSICS**

Concept-Development Practice Page   **10-1**

Center of Gravity

1. Which bottle is the most stable?_____

       least stable?_____

       neutral?_____

2. Draw vectors for the weight of each truck. Which truck will tip over? _____

   Why? _____

   _____

3. Both blocks have equal mass. Which requires more work to tip over? _____

   Why? _____

   _____

4. Why or why not will the pipe tip over?

   _____

   _____

5. The wheels of a bike provide two points of contact with the ground. A kick stand provides a third. Sketch in the triangular area bounded by the three points of ground contact. Where is the CG of the bike with respect to this area?

   _____

   _____

Conceptual **PHYSICS**

6. Ordinarily when you stand with your back and heels to a wall, you cannot bend over and touch your toes without toppling forward. Why?

_____

But if you stand with your back and heels to the slanted wall below, you *can* lean over and touch your toes without toppling. Complete the sketch to the right to show how.

7. A person stands upright without difficulty. On each of the sketches below, draw the weight vector and show why the same person cannot stand on tiptoes against the wall.

**Concept-Development
Practice Page**   **11-1**

Torques

1. Apply what you know about torques by making a mobile. Shown below are five horizontal arms with fixed 1- and 2-kg masses attached, and four hangers with ends that fit in the loops of the arms, lettered A through R. You are to figure where the loops should be attached so that when the whole system is suspended from the spring scale at the top, it will hang as a proper mobile, with its arms suspended horizontally. This is best done by working from the bottom upward. Circle the loops where the hangers should be attached. When the mobile is complete, how many kilograms will be indicated on the scale? (Assume the horizontal struts and connecting hooks are practically massless compared to the 1- and 2-kg masses.) On a separate sheet of paper, make a sketch of your completed mobile.

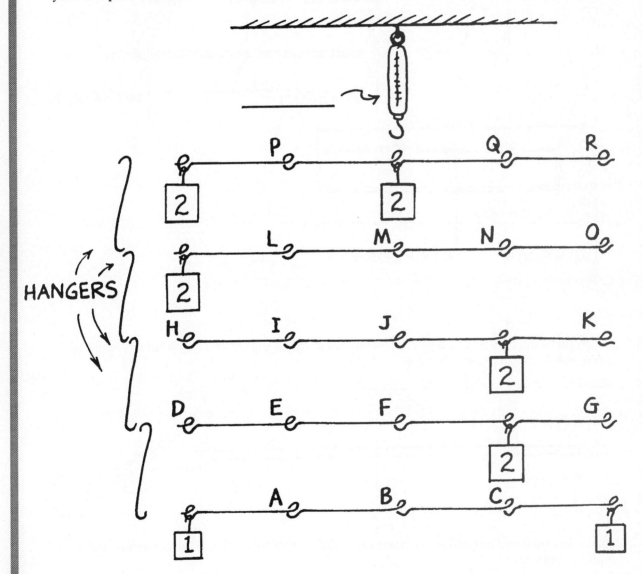

2. Complete the data for the three seesaws in equilibrium.

3. The broom balances at its CG. If you cut the broom in half at the CG and weigh each part of the broom, which end would weigh more?

_____

Explain why each end has or does not have the same weight? (Hint: Compare this to one of the seesaw systems above.)

_____

_____

Torques

Health-Spa physics!

1. Felix Flex pulls the bar forward, rotates the cam, and lifts the load. Two torques act on the cam—the counter-clockwise torque produced by Felix's pull **P**, and the clockwise torque produced by the tension **T** that supports the load: Note that although **T** stays constant, the torque is not constant because of the variable lever arm (hence the cam's odd shape!).

Shown below is the cam in three positions, A, B, and C. The lever arm (heavy dashed line) is shown for position A.

a. Draw the different-length lever arms for positions B and C. (Take care that your lever arm is perpendicular to the line of action of T!)

The cam provides a changing lever arm!

b. In which position does the cam provide the longest lever arm? _____

c. In which position does **T** produce the greatest torque? _____

d. In which position does the cam provide the shortest lever arm? _____

e. In which position does **T** produce the least torque? _____

f. Which position requires the least pull **P** for Felix to rotate? _____

g. Which position requires the most pull **P** for Felix to rotate? _____

Note that (**P** x lever arm between **P** and cam axis) = (**T** x lever arm you constructed in a)

Tension **T** = weight of the load, whether the load is held stationary or moved at constant speed.

The torque Felix produces on the cam depends on his pull **P**, which in turn depends on the cam position.

Conceptual PHYSICS

thanx to Manuel Hewitt

2. Pull the string gently and the spool rolls. The direction of roll depends on the way the torque is applied.

In (1) and (2) below, the force and lever arm are shown for the torque about the point where surface contact is made (shown by the triangular "fulcrum").The lever arm is the heavy dashed line, which is different for each different pulling position.

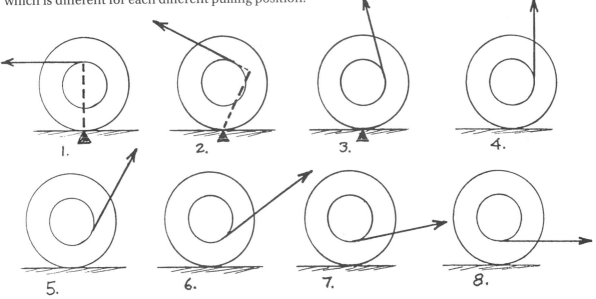

1. 2. 3. 4.

5. 6. 7. 8.

a. Construct the lever arm for the other positions.

b. Lever arm is longer when the string is on the (top) (bottom) of the spool spindle.

c. For a given pull, the torque is greater when the string is on the (top) (bottom).

d. For the same pull, rotational acceleration is greater when the string is on

   (top) (bottom) (makes no difference).

e. At which positions does the spool roll to the left? _____

f. At which positions does the spool roll to the right? _____

g. At which position does the spool not roll at all? _____

h. Why does the spool slide rather than roll at this position?

> Be sure your right angle is between the force's _line of action_ and the lever arm.

_____

3. We all know that a ball rolls down an incline. But relatively few people know that the reason the ball picks up rotational speed is because of a torque. In Sketch A, we see the ingredients of the torque acting on the ball—the force due to gravity and the lever arm to the point where surface contact is made.

a. Constuct the lever arms for positions B and C.

b. As the incline becomes steeper, the torque

   (increases) (decreases) (remains the same).

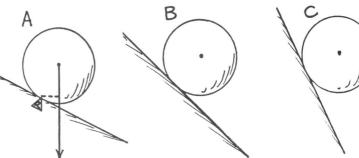

A   B   C

Inverse–Square Law

1. Paint spray travels radially away from the nozzle of the can in straight lines. Like gravity, the strength (intensity) of the spray obeys an inverse-square law. Complete the diagram by filling in the blank spaces.

	1 AREA UNIT	4 AREA UNITS	( ) AREA UNITS	( ) AREA UNITS
PAINT SPRAY	1 mm THICK	¼ mm THICK	( ) mm THICK	( ) mm THICK

2. A small light source located 1 m in front of an opening of area 1 m² illuminates a wall behind. If the wall is 1 m behind the opening (2 m from the light source), the illuminated area covers 4 m². How many square meters will be illuminated if the wall is

   5 m from the source? _____

   10 m from the source? _____

3. Hold your hands outstretched, one twice as far from your eyes as the other, and make a casual judgment as to which hand looks bigger. Most people see them to be about the same size, while many see the nearer hand as slightly bigger. Almost nobody upon casual inspection sees the nearer hand as four times as big. But because your vision depends upon an inverse-square law, the nearer hand should appear twice as tall and twice as wide, and therefore occupy four times as much of your visual field, as the farther hand. Your belief that your hands are the same size is so strong that you likely overrule this information. Now if you overlap your hands slightly and view them with one eye closed, you'll see the nearer hand as clearly bigger. This raises an interesting question: What other illusions do you have that are not so easily checked?

Conceptual **PHYSICS**

Force and Weight

1. An apple that has a mass of 0.1 kilogram has the same mass wherever it is. The amount of matter that makes up the apple

    (depends upon)   (does not depend upon)

    the location of the apple. It has the same resistance to acceleration wherever it is — its inertia everywhere is

    (the same)   (different).

    The weight of the apple is a different story. It may weigh exactly 1 N in San Francisco and slightly less in mile-high Denver, Colorado. On the surface of the moon the apple would weigh 1/6 N, and far out in outer space it may have almost no weight at all. The quantity that doesn't change with location is

    (mass)   (weight),

    and the quantity that may change with location is its

    (mass)   (weight).

    That's because

    (mass)   (weight)

    is the force due to gravity on a body, and this force varies with distance. So weight is the force of gravity between two bodies, usually some small object in contact with the earth. When we refer to the

    (mass)   (weight)

    of an object we are usually speaking of the gravitational force that attracts it to the earth.

Fill in the blanks:

2. If we stand on a weighing scale and find that we are pulled toward the earth with a force of 500 N, then we weigh _____ N. Strictly speaking, we weigh _____ N relative to the earth. How much does the earth weigh? If we tip the scale upside down and repeat the weighing process, we can say that we and the earth are still pulled together with a force of _____ N, and therefore, relative to us, the whole 6 000 000 000 000 000 000 000 000-kg earth weighs _____ N! Weight, unlike mass, is a relative quantity.

> VIEW THE SAME FROM ANOTHER PERSPECTIVE!

> DO YOU SEE WHY IT MAKES SENSE TO DISCUSS THE EARTH'S MASS, BUT NOT ITS WEIGHT?

We are pulled to the earth with a force of 500 N, so we weigh 500 N.

The earth is pulled toward us with a force of 500 N, so it weighs 500 N.

Conceptual PHYSICS

3. The spaceship is attracted to both the planet and the planet's moon. The planet has four times the mass of its moon. The force of attraction of the spaceship to the planet is shown by the vector.

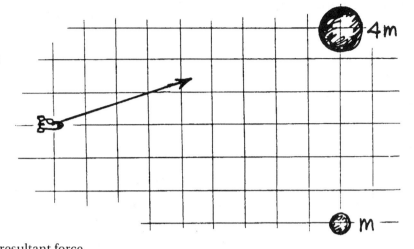

a. Carefully sketch another vector to show the spaceship's attraction to the moon. Then use the parallelogram method of Chapter 6 and sketch the resultant force.

b. Determine the location between the planet and its moon (along the dotted line) where gravitational forces cancel. Make a sketch of the spaceship there.

4. Consider a planet of uniform density that has a straight tunnel from the north pole through the center to the south pole. At the surface of the planet, an object weighs 1 ton.

a. Fill in the gravitational force on the object when it is half way to the center, then at the center.

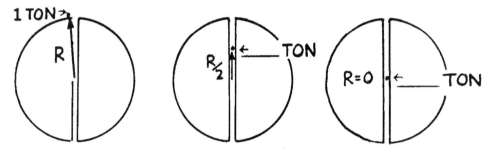

b. Describe the motion you would experience if you fell into the tunnel.

_____

5. Consider an object that weighs 1 ton at the surface of a planet, just before the planet gravitationally collapses. (The mass of the planet remains the same during collapse.)

a. Fill in the weights of the object on the planet's shrinking surface at the radial values shown.

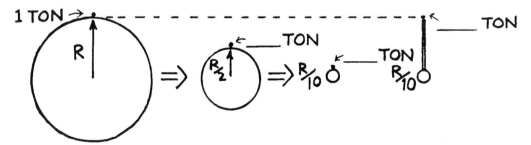

b. When the planet has collapsed to 1/10 of its initial radius, a ladder is erected that puts the object as far from its center as the object was originally. Fill in its weight at this position.

Conceptual **PHYSICS**

Concept-Development Practice Page **13-2**

Gravitational Interactions

The equation for the law of universal gravitation is

$$F = G \frac{m_1 m_2}{d^2}$$

where F is the attractive force between masses m_1 and m_2 separated by distance d. G is the universal gravitational constant (and relates G to the masses and distance as the constant π similarly relates the circumference of a circle to its diameter). By substituting changes in any of the variables into this equation, we can predict how the others change. For example, we can see how the force changes if we know how either or both of the masses change, or how the distance between their centers changes.

Suppose, for example, that one of the masses somehow is doubled. Then substituting $2m_1$ for m_1 in the equation gives

$$F_{NEW} = G \frac{2m_1 m_2}{d^2} = 2\left(G \frac{m_1 m_2}{d^2}\right) = 2F_{OLD}$$

So we see the force doubles also. Or suppose instead that the distance of separation is doubled. Then substituting $2d$ for d in the equation gives

$$F_{NEW} = G \frac{m_1 m_2}{(2d)^2} = G \frac{m_1 m_2}{4d^2} = \frac{1}{4}\left(G \frac{m_1 m_2}{d^2}\right) = \frac{1}{4} F_{OLD}$$

And we see the force is only 1/4 as much.

Use this method to solve the following problems. Write the equation and make the appropriate substitutions.

1. If both masses are doubled, what happens to the force?

2. If the masses are not changed, but the distance of separation is reduced to 1/2 the original distance, what happens to the force?

GRAVITY
:SIGH:

Conceptual PHYSICS

3. If the masses are not changed, but the distance of separation is reduced to 1/4 the original distance, what happens to the force?

4. If both masses are doubled, and the distance of separation is doubled, show what happens to the force.

5. If one of the masses is doubled, the other remains unchanged, and the distance of separation is tripled, show what happens to the force.

6. Consider a pair of binary stars that pull on each other with a certain force. Would the force be larger or smaller if the mass of each star were three times as great when their distance apart is three times as far? Show what the new force will be compared to the first one.

**Concept-Development
Practice Page**   **13-3**

Our Ocean Tides

1. Consider two equal-mass blobs of water, A and B, initially at rest in the moon's gravitational field. The vector shows the gravitational force of the moon on A.

a. Draw a force vector on B due to the moon's gravity.

b. Is the force on B more or less than the force on A? _____

c. Why?_____

d. The blobs accelerate toward the moon. Which has the greater acceleration? (A) (B)

e. Because of the different accelerations, with time

(A gets farther ahead of B) (A and B gain identical speeds) and the distance between A and B

(increases) (stays the same) (decreases).

f. If A and B were connected by a rubber band, with time the rubber band would

(stretch) (not stretch).

g. This (stretching) (non-stretching) is due to the (difference) (non-difference) in the moon's gravitational pulls.

h. The two blobs will eventually crash into the moon. To orbit around the moon instead of crashing into it, the blobs should move

(away from the moon) (tangentially). Then their accelerations will consist of changes in

(speed) (direction).

2. Now consider the same two blobs located on opposite sides of the earth.

 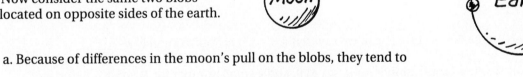

a. Because of differences in the moon's pull on the blobs, they tend to

(spread away from each other) (approach each other).

b. Does this spreading produce ocean tides? (Yes) (No)

c. If earth and moon were closer, gravitational force between them would be

(more) (the same) (less), and the difference in gravitational forces on the near and far parts

of the ocean would be (more) (the same) (less).

d. Because the earth's orbit about the sun is slightly elliptical, earth and sun are closer in December

than in June. Taking the sun's tidal force into account, on a world average, ocean tides are greater in

(December) (June) (no difference).

Conceptual **PHYSICS**

Tidal Gravity

This supplements the Plug & Chugs and Think & Solves in the textbook, Chapter 13, to show how tides vary with the inverse cube of distance. Unlike other Practice Pages, this one is more algebra than physics.

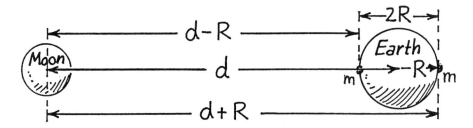

Consider the gravitational interaction between the moon and two small blobs of water, each with the same mass m, on opposite sides of the earth. The nearest blob to the moon is pulled by the moon's gravity with a force $F_1 = \dfrac{GMm}{(d-R)^2}$, where m is the mass of the blob of water, M is the mass of the moon, d is the distance from the center of the moon to the center of the earth, and R is the radius of the earth (so $d - R$ is the distance from the moon's center to the near blob of water). On the far side of the earth, a blob of water of the same mass m is attracted by the moon with a force $F_2 = \dfrac{GMm}{(d+R)^2}$.

1. Which of these two forces is stronger, and why? _____.

2. The difference in these two forces, $\Delta F = F_1 - F_2$, produces tides. With a bit of algebra, on a separate sheet of paper, subtract F_2 from F_1.

   Noting that $(d-R)(d+R) = d^2 - R^2$, see that your answer can be expressed $\Delta F = \dfrac{4GMmdR}{(d^2-R^2)^2}$.

3. If d is very much larger than R, can we say that $(d^2 - R^2)$ is approximately d^2?_____

   (Hint: substitute a large number for d, say 100, and a small number for R, say 1.)

4. With this approximation, show that the above equation in #2 is very nearly $\Delta F = \dfrac{4GMmR}{d^3}$.

5. "Tidal Force" T_F is the difference in force per unit mass acting on the water blobs. Show that $T_F = \dfrac{\Delta F}{m} = \dfrac{4GMR}{d^3}$.

6. Show with units analysis that T_F has units newtons per kilogram.

Now have a go at the Plug & Chugs and Think & Solves of Chapter 13 in the textbook.

Satellite Motion

1. Figure A shows "Newton's Mountain," so high that its top is above the drag of the atmosphere. The cannonball is fired and hits the ground as shown.

    a. You draw the path the cannonball might take if it were fired a little bit faster.

    b. Repeat for a still greater speed, but still less than 8 km/s.

    c. Then draw the orbital path it would take if its speed were 8 km/s.

    d. What is the shape of the 8 km/s curve?

    _____

    Figure A

    e. What would be the shape of the orbital path if the cannonball were fired at a speed of about 9 km/s?

    _____

2. Figure B shows a satellite in circular orbit.

    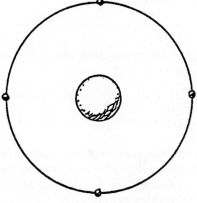

    a. At each of the four positions draw a vector that represents the gravitational *force* exerted on the satellite.

    b. Label the force vectors *F*.

    c. Then draw at each position a vector to represent the *velocity* of the satellite at that position, and label it *V*.

    d. Are all four *F* vectors the same length? Why or why not?

    _____

    Figure B

    e. Are all four *V* vectors the same length? Why or why not?

    _____

    f. What is the angle between your *F* and *V* vectors? _____

    g. Is there any component of *F* along *V*? _____

    h. What does this tell you about the work the force of gravity does on the satellite?

    _____

    i. Does the KE of the satellite in Figure B remain constant, or does it vary? _____

    j. Does the PE of the satellite remain constant, or does it vary?

    _____

Conceptual PHYSICS

3. Figure C shows a satellite in elliptical orbit.

a. Repeat the procedure you used for the circular orbit, drawing vectors *F* and *V* for each position, including proper labeling. Show equal magnitudes with equal lengths, and greater magnitudes with greater lengths, but don't bother making the scale accurate.

b. Are your vectors *F* all the same magnitude? Why or why not?

_____

_____

c. Are your vectors *V* all the same magnitude? Why or why not?

_____

_____

_____

_____

d. Is the angle between vectors *F* and *V* everywhere the same, or does it vary?

_____

e. Are there places where there is a component of *F* along *V*?

_____

_____

f. Is work done on the satellite when there is a component of *F* along and in the same direction of *V* and if so, does this increase or decrease the KE of the satellite?

_____

g. When there is a component of *F* along and opposite to the direction of *V*, does this increase or decrease the KE of the satellite?

_____

_____

_____

h. What can you say about the sum KE + PE along the orbit?

_____

_____

Figure C

Conceptual **PHYSICS**

Special Relativity–Space and Time

Section 15.7, *The Twin-Trip,* compares the times experienced by a traveling twin and a stay-at-home twin. The 2-hour trip experienced by the traveling twin is observed to take 2.5 hours from a frame of reference on earth, as evidenced by the sending and receiving of regularly-spaced flashes of light. The 6-minute-interval flashes emitted by the spaceship are seen from earth at 12-minute intervals when the spaceship is leaving the earth, and at 3-minute intervals when the spaceship is approaching the earth. Read the textbook carefully and fill in the readings on the spaceship clock below for each flash emitted, and on the earth clock for each flash received.

SHIP LEAVING EARTH

FLASH	TIME ON ROCKET WHEN FLASH SENT	TIME ON EARTH WHEN FLASH SEEN
0	12:00	12:00
1	12:06	
2		
3		
4		
5		
6		
7		
8		
9		
10		

SHIP APPROACHING EARTH

FLASH	TIME ON ROCKET WHEN FLASH SENT	TIME ON EARTH WHEN FLASH SEEN
11		
12		
13		
14		
15		
16		
17		
18		
19		
20		

The fact that the clocks read differently when each is in a different realm of spacetime is a consequence of differences in

    (the clock mechanisms)   (time itself)

Conceptual PHYSICS

Special Relativity – Length, Momentum, and Energy

1. Pretend we are on a space mission to Jupiter. Our instruments detect an identical sister space station, Alpha Alberta, moving away from us at 80% of the speed of light. Our instruments reveal that, compared to our station,

   a. clocks and events on Alpha Alberta are

     (slow) (fast) (the same)

   b. the length of Alpha Alberta in its direction of motion appears

     (shorter) (longer) (the same)

   c. the momentum of Alpha Alberta is

     (more) (less) (the same)

Occupants on Alpha Alberta are making measurements of us. They observe that, compared to their station,

   d. clocks and events on our space station are

     (slow) (fast) (the same)

   e. the length of our space station is

     (shorter) (longer) (the same)

   f. our momentum is

     (more) (less) (the same)

2. A gram of water has a volume of 1 cubic centimeter, about the size of a sugar cube. A gram of iron has a smaller volume, about the size of a pea, and a gram of platinum is even smaller, about the size of a small raisin. In a gram of any kind of matter is an equivalent vast amount of rest energy. We can see how much energy a gram of matter is equal to in joules from the celebrated equation $E_0 = mc^2$, where $m = 1\ g = 10^{-3}\ kg$, and $c = 3 \times 10^8\ m/s$. Then

$$E_0 = mc^2 = (10^{-3}\ kg)(3 \times 10^8\ m/s)2 = 9 \times 10^{13}\ J$$

BURN 15,000 BARRELS OF OIL AND YOU EQUAL THE ENERGY EQUIVALENT OF ANY GRAM OF MATTER!

In comparison, one barrel of crude oil when burned yields $6 \times 10^9\ J$. According to this data, is the statement by the man at the right an overestimate, an underestimate, or accurate? Defend your answer.

_____

_____

Conceptual **PHYSICS**

Mechanics Overview

1. The sketch shows the elliptical path described by a satellite about the earth. In which of the marked positions, A - D, (put S for "same everywhere") does the satellite experience the maximum

   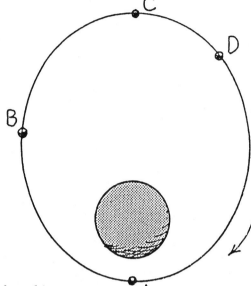

   a. gravitational force?_____

   b. speed? _____

   c. momentum?_____

   d. kinetic energy?_____

   e. gravitational potential energy?_____

   f. total energy (KE + PE)?_____

   g. acceleration?_____

   h. angular momentum?_____

2. Answer the above questions for a satellite in circular orbit.

   a. _____ b._____ c._____ d._____ e._____ f. _____ g._____ h._____

3. In which position(s) is there momentarily no work being done on the satellite by the force of gravity? Why?

   _____

4. Work changes energy. Let the equation for work, $W = Fd$, guide your thinking on these: Defend your answers in terms of $W = Fd$.

   a. In which position will a several-minutes thrust of rocket engines pushing the satellite forward do the most work on the satellite and give it the greatest change in kinetic energy? (Hint: think about where the most distance will be traveled during the application of a several-minutes thrust?)

   _____

   b. In which position will a several-minutes thrust of rocket engines pushing the satellite forward do the least work on the satellite and give it the least boost in kinetic energy?

   _____

   c. In which positon will a several-minutes thrust of a retro-rocket (pushing opposite to the satellite's direction of motion) do the most work on the satellite and change its kinetic energy the most?

   _____

Conceptual **PHYSICS**

The Atomic Nature of Matter

ATOMS ARE CLASSIFIED BY THEIR ATOMIC NUMBER, WHICH IS THE SAME AS THE NUMBER OF _____ IN THE NUCLEUS.

TO CHANGE THE ATOMS OF ONE ELEMENT INTO THOSE OF ANOTHER, _____ MUST BE ADDED OR SUBTRACTED!

Use the periodic table on page 254 of your text to help you answer the following questions.

1. When the atomic nuclei of hydrogen and lithium are squashed together (nuclear fusion) the element that is produced is

   _____

2. When the atomic nuclei of a pair of lithium nuclei are fused, the element produced is

   _____

3. When the atomic nuclei of a pair of aluminum nuclei are fused, the element produced is

   _____

4. When the nucleus of a nitrogen atom absorbs a proton, the resulting element is

   _____

5. What element is produced when a gold nucleus gains a proton?

   _____

6. Which results in the more valuable product – *adding* or *subtracting* protons from gold nuclei?

   _____

   _____

7. What element is produced when a uranium nucleus ejects an elementary particle composed of two protons and two neutrons?

   _____

8. If a uranium nucleus breaks into two pieces (nuclear fission) and one of the pieces is zirconium (atomic number 40), the other piece is the element

   _____

9. Which has more mass, a nitrogen molecule (N_2) or an oxygen molecule (O_2)?

   _____

10. Which has the greater number of atoms, a gram of helium or a gram of neon?

    _____

I LIKE THE WAY YOUR ATOMS ARE PUT TOGETHER!

SIGH

Conceptual PHYSICS

Concept-Development Practice Page **18-1**

Scaling Squares

1. If you have a square 1 cm on each side, what is its area? _____cm^2

A SQUARE OF SIDE ℓ HAS AN AREA ℓ^2

2. If you have a square 2 cm on each side, what is its area? _____cm^2

3. Consider a square piece of pizza, 10 cm x 10 cm. Another piece of pizza measures 20 cm x 20 cm. How does the area of the larger pizza compare?

_____

4. If you have a square 4 cm on each side, what is its area? _____ cm^2

5. If you have a square 10 cm on each side, what is its area? _____ cm^2

6. If you double each side of a square, how many times as large does its area become?

_____

7. If you triple each side of a square, how many times as large does its area become?

_____

8. *True or false:* If the side of a square is increased by a certain factor, say 5, then the area increases by the *square* of the factor, in this case 5^2 (or 25). _____

   So, if you scale up the side of a square by a factor of 10, its area will increase by a factor of _____, or _____.

WHEN YOU DOUBLE THE SIDE OF A SQUARE, YOU GET _____ TIMES THE AREA

AND IF YOU TRIPLE THE SIDE OF A SQUARE YOU GET _____ TIMES THE AREA

IN GENERAL, IF YOU X THE SIDE OF A SQUARE, YOU X^2 THE AREA !

Conceptual PHYSICS

Scaling Circles

1. Complete the table.

CIRCLES		
RADIUS	CIRCUMFERENCE	AREA
1 cm	$2\pi(1cm) = 2\pi$ cm	$\pi(1cm)^2 = \pi cm^2$
2 cm		
3 cm		
10 cm		

FOR THE CIRCUMFERENCE OF A CIRCLE, $C = 2\pi r$

AND FOR THE AREA OF A CIRCLE, $A = \pi r^2$

2. From your completed table, when the radius of a circle is doubled, its area increases by a factor of _____. When the radius is increased by a factor of 10, the area increases by a factor of _____.

3. Consider a round pizza that costs $2.00. Another pizza of the same thickness has twice the diameter. How much should the larger pizza cost?

_____

4. *True or false*: If the radius of a circle is increased by a certain factor, say 5, then the area increases by the *square* of the factor, in this case 5^2 or 25. _____

So if you scale up the radius of a circle by a factor of 10, its area will increase by a factor of _____.

5. *(Application:)* Suppose you raise chickens and spend $50 to buy wire for a chicken pen. To hold the most chickens inside, you should make the shape of the pen

    (square) (circular) (either, for both provide the same area)

**Concept-Development
Practice Page** 18-2

Scaling Cubes

1. Consider a cube, say 1 cm x 1 cm x 1 cm (about the size of a sugar cube). Its volume is 1 cm³. The surface area of one of its faces is 1 cm². This is also the area of any cross-section (a slice through the cube that is parallel to any of its faces). The total surface area of the cube is 6 cm², because it has 6 faces (4 sides and top and bottom; count them).

Now consider a second cube, scaled up ay a factor of 2 so it is 2 cm x 2 cm x 2 cm.

a. What is the total surface areas of each cube?

1st cube_____ cm²; 2nd cube_____ cm²

b. How many times more is the total surface area of the second cube compared to that of the first?

_____

c. What are the volumes of the cubes?

1st cube _____ cm³; 2nd cube _____ cm³

d. How many times more is the volume of the second cube compared to that of the first?

_____

e. Compare the surface-area-to-volume ratio fo

1st cube: $\dfrac{\text{surface area}}{\text{volume}}$ = _____   2nd cube: $\dfrac{\text{surface area}}{\text{volume}}$ = _____

2. As the size of a cube (or object of any shape) increases, the ratio of surface area to volume decreases. This means that the gain in surface area is proportionally less than the gain in volume (area gains only as the *square* of the increase, while volume gains as the *cube* of the increase). Apply this relationship and good thinking to explain the following:

a. Why does a cup of coffee cool faster than the pot from which it is poured? Or, if you want your coffee to stay warm, should you pour it into a cup or leave it in the pot? Explain.

_____

_____

b. Chickens, Cornish game hens, and turkeys have approximately the same body shape. If you had two birds, one with a body twice as wide, twice as thick, and twice as long, how would you expect their weights to compare? How about the amounts of skin?

_____

_____

Conceptual PHYSICS

Scaling Solids

1. a. Consider a pair of cubes, each 1 cm on a side. The volume of each cube is _____ cm³, so the total volume of both cubes is _____ cm³. The total surface area of each cube is _____ cm², so the total surface area of both cubes is _____ cm².

    b. If the two cubes are glued together, to make a double cube, the total volume is _____ cm³ and the total exposed surface area is _____ cm².

2. The sketch to the right is a scaled-up version of the small double cube. It is scaled up by a factor of 2 (twice as wide, twice as thick, and twice as tall).

    a. Its volume is _____ cm³.

    b. Its total surface area is _____ cm².

    c. Which has the greater surface-area-to-volume ratio, the small or the scaled-up double cube?

    _____ _____

    _____

3. Scale up the double cube of Question 2 by a factor of 3 (three times as tall and three times as wide both ways). Make a sketch of it in the space at the right.

    a. Its volume is _____ cm³.

    b. Its total surface area is _____ cm².

    c. Which of the three versions of the double cube has the most surface area? _____

    d. Which has the most surface area compared to its volume?

    _____

4. *True or false:* As the volume of an object increases, its surface area also increases, but the ratio of surface area to volume decreases._____

5. The effects of scaling are good for some creatures and bad for others. Write either good (G) or bad (B) for each of the following:

    a. An insect falling from a tall tree ____   b. An elephant falling from the same tree ____

    c. A small fish trying to flee a big fish ____   d. A big fish chasing a small fish ____

    e. An insect that falls in the water ____   f. A hungry sparrow ____

Conceptual **PHYSICS**

Name _____   Period _____   Date _____

**Concept-Development
Practice Page** **19–1**

Archimedes' Principle I

1. Consider a balloon filled with 1 liter of water (1000 cm³) in equilibrium in a container of water, as shown in Figure 1.

$1000 cm^3 = 1 g/cm^3$ $m = pv$

   a. What is the mass of the 1 liter of water? $P = \frac{m}{V}$

      _____ $1000g = 1 kg$ _____

   b. What is the weight of the 1 liter of water?

      _____ $9.81 \times 1kg = 9.81N$ _____

   c. What is the weight of water displaced by the balloon?

      _____ $9.81N$ _____

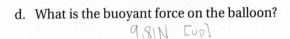
$\vec{F_b} = V_{05} \cdot P_{fluid} \cdot g = 9.81N$

$(1000 cm^3)(\frac{0.001 kg}{cm^3})(9.81 \frac{m}{s})$

   d. What is the buoyant force on the balloon?

      _____ $9.81N \;[up]$ _____

   e. Sketch a pair of vectors in Figure 1: one for the weight of the balloon and the other for the buoyant force that acts on it. How do the size and directions of your vectors compare?

      _____ Same size but opposite direction _____

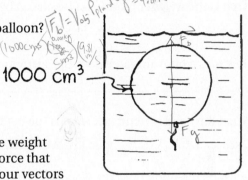

WATER DOES NOT SINK IN WATER !

1000 cm³ ⟶

Figure 1

2. As a thought experiment, pretend we could remove the water from the balloon but still have it remain the same size of 1 liter. Then inside the balloon is a vacuum.

   a. What is the mass of the liter of nothing?

      _____ $0 kg$ _____

   b. What is the weight of the liter of nothing?

      _____ $0 kg$ _____

   c. What is the weight of water displaced by the massless balloon?

      _____ $9.81N$ _____

   d. What is the buoyant force on the massless balloon?

      _____ $9.81N \;[up]$ _____

ANYTHING THAT DISPLACES 9.8 N OF WATER EXPERIENCES 9.8 N OF BUOYANT FORCE.

CUZ IF YOU PUSH 9.8 N OF WATER ASIDE THE WATER PUSHES BACK ON YOU WITH 9.8 N !

   e. In which direction would the massless balloon be accelerated?

      _____ up _____

Conceptual PHYSICS

     Chapter 19   Liquids   **69**

3. Assume the balloon is replaced by a 0.5-kilogram piece of wood that has exactly the same volume (1000 cm³), as shown in Figure 2. The wood is held in the same submerged position beneath the surface of the water.

   a. What volume of water is displaced by the wood?

   _____ 1 L   (1000 cm³) _____

   b. What is the mass of the water displaced by the wood?

   _____ 1 kg _____

   c. What is the weight of the water displaced by the wood?

   _____ 9.8 N _____

   d. How much buoyant force does the surrounding water exert on the wood?

   _____ 9.8 N [up] _____

   e. When the hand is removed, what is the net force on the wood?

   _____ 9.8 N + −4.9 N = 4.9 N _____

   f. In which direction does the wood accelerate when released? ___ up _____

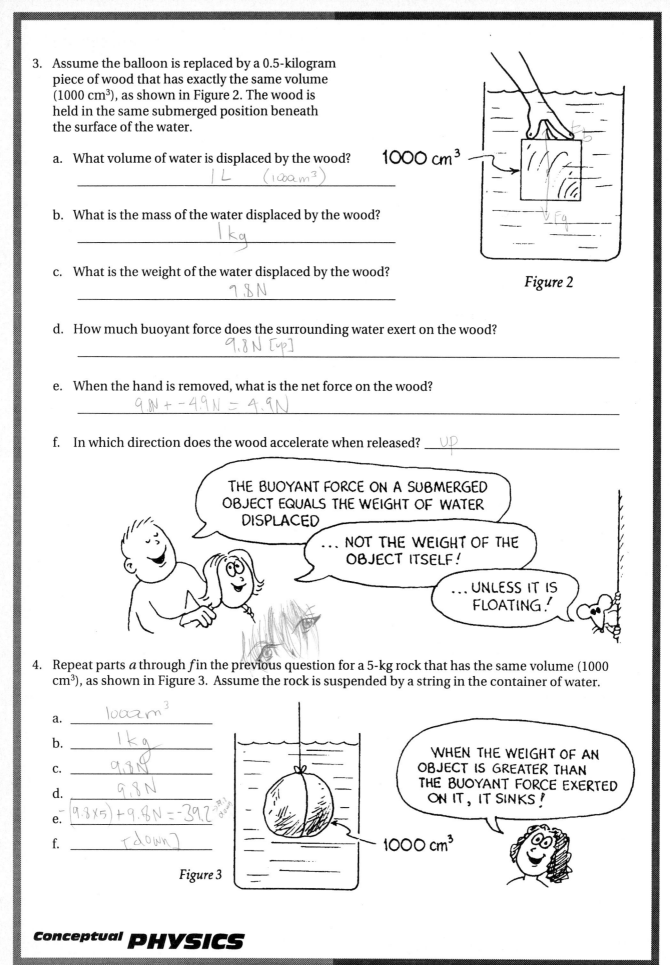

1000 cm³

Figure 2

THE BUOYANT FORCE ON A SUBMERGED OBJECT EQUALS THE WEIGHT OF WATER DISPLACED

... NOT THE WEIGHT OF THE OBJECT ITSELF!

... UNLESS IT IS FLOATING!

4. Repeat parts *a* through *f* in the previous question for a 5-kg rock that has the same volume (1000 cm³), as shown in Figure 3. Assume the rock is suspended by a string in the container of water.

   a. _____ 1000 cm³ _____
   b. _____ 1 kg _____
   c. _____ 9.8 N _____
   d. _____ 9.8 N _____
   e. _____ (9.8 × 5) + 9.8 N = −39.2 ₋₃₉.₂ down _____
   f. _____ [down] _____

   Figure 3

   1000 cm³

   WHEN THE WEIGHT OF AN OBJECT IS GREATER THAN THE BUOYANT FORCE EXERTED ON IT, IT SINKS!

Conceptual **PHYSICS**

**Concept-Development
Practice Page** **19–2**

Archimedes' Principle II

1. The water lines for the first three cases are shown. Sketch in the appropriate water lines for cases *d* and *e*, and make up your own for case *f*.

a. DENSER THAN WATER   b. SAME DENSITY AS WATER   c. 1/2 AS DENSE AS WATER

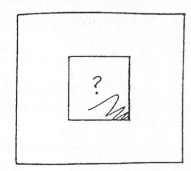

d. 1/4 AS DENSE AS WATER   e. 3/4 AS DENSE AS WATER   f._____AS DENSE AS WATER

2. ___ If the weight of a ship is 100 million N, then the water it displaces weighs_____ .

   If cargo weighing 1000 N is put on board then the ship will sink down until an extra

   _____ of water is displaced.

3. The first two sketches below show the water line for an empty and a loaded ship. Draw in the appropriate water line for the third sketch.

a. SHIP EMPTY   b. SHIP LOADED WITH 50 TONS OF IRON   c. SHIP LOADED WITH 50 TONS OF STYROFOAM

Conceptual PHYSICS

4. Here is a glass of ice water with an ice cube floating in it. Draw the water line after the ice cube melts. (Will the water line rise, fall, or remain the same?)

_____

_____

_____

_____

_____

5. The air-filled balloon is weighted so it sinks in water. Near the surface, the balloon has a certain volume. Draw the balloon at the bottom (inside the dashed square) and show whether it is bigger, smaller, or the same size.

a. Since the weighted balloon sinks, how does its overall density compare to the density of water?

_____

b. As the weighted balloon sinks, does its density increase, decrease, or remain the same?

_____

c. Since the weighted balloon sinks, how does the buoyant force on it compare to its weight?

_____

d. As the weighted balloon sinks deeper, does the buoyant force on it increase, decrease, or remain the same?

_____

5. What would be your answers to Questions *a, b, c,* and *d* for a rock instead of an air-filled balloon?

a. _____

b. _____

c. _____

d. _____

Conceptual PHYSICS

Gases

1. A principle difference between a liquid and a gas is that when a liquid is under pressure, its volume

    (increases)   (decreases)   (doesn't change noticeably)

    and its density

    (increases)   (decreases)   (doesn't change noticeably)

    When a gas is under pressure, its volume

    (increases)   (decreases)   (doesn't change noticeably)

    and its density

    (increases)   (decreases)   (doesn't change noticeably)

2. The sketch shows the launching of a weather balloon at sea level. Make a sketch of the same weather balloon when it is high in the atmosphere. In words, what is different about its size and why?

    _____

    _____

    _____

    _____

HIGH-ALTITUDE SIZE

GROUND-LEVEL SIZE

3. A hydrogen-filled balloon that weighs 10 N must displace_____N of air in order to float in air.

    If it displaces less than_____N it will be buoyed up with less than_____N and sink.

    If it displaces more than_____N of air it will move upward.

4. Why is the cartoon more humorous to physics types than to non-physics types? What physics has occurred?

    _____

    _____

    _____

    _____

RATS TO YOU TOO, DANIEL BERNOULLI!

Conceptual **PHYSICS**

Syringes and Vacuum Pumps

The old fashioned farm-type pump shown in Figure 20.9 in your text is a *lift pump* that operates by atmospheric pressure. Its operation is similar to that of a common *syringe* (the device that holds the needle your doctor or dentist uses, or the gadget inside a toy water pistol).

1. The nozzle of the syringe is held beneath the surface of water in Figure A. When the piston is pulled up, water fills the nozzle and the chamber under the piston.

   Figure A

   a. What forces water into the nozzle and chamber?

      _____

      _____

   b. When the syringe is removed from the water and held in the air, the water doesn't leak out. Why?

      _____

      _____

   c. Would water leak out if air leaked past the piston? Explain briefly.

      _____

      _____

      _____

   d. What happens if the piston is pushed down? (Do you see how water pistols work?)

      _____

      _____

      _____

2. A lift pump is like a syringe with two valves. Valve A is like a little door that lets water come up but will not let water go down again. Valve B is in the piston; it also lets water come up but not down again. In Figure B, both valves are closed and there are no regions of reduced air pressure.

   Figure B

Figure C   Figure D   Figure E

When the piston is raised (Figure C), air pressure is reduced in the pipe that extends into the water. This allows water from below to be pushed up into the pipe by

(atmospheric pressure)   (a vacuum).

Valve A opens as water enters the chamber. When the piston is pushed down (Figure D), valve A closes and valve B

(closes also)   (opens).

This lets water enter the chamber above the piston. When the piston is lifted again (Figure E), Valve B

(closes)   (opens)

and water is lifted to flow

(out of the pump)   (back into the pipe).

3. Under ideal conditions and a perfect vacuum, what is the maximum height that water at sea level can be lifted in this manner?

_____

4. Would this maximum height be greater or less for a lift pump high in the mountains? Defend your answer.

_____

Conceptual **PHYSICS**

Concept-Development Practice Page   **21-1**

Temperature, Heat, and Expansion

1. Complete the table:

TEMPERATURE OF MELTING ICE	0 °C	32 °F	273.15 K
TEMPERATURE OF BOILING WATER	100 °C	212 °F	373.15 K

2. Suppose you apply a flame and heat one liter of water, raising its temperature 10°C. If you transfer the same heat energy to two liters, how much will the temperature rise? For three liters? *Record your answers on the blanks in the drawing at the right.*

$\Delta T = \dfrac{Q}{cm} = 4800$

$\Delta T = 10°C$ $\Delta T = 5 °C$ $\Delta T = 3.3 °C$

3. A thermometer is in a container half-filled with 20°C water.

  a. When an equal volume of 20°C water is added, the temperature of the mixture is

    (10°C) (20°C) (40°C)

  b. When instead an equal volume of 40°C water is added, the temperature of the mixture will be

    (20°C) (30°C) (40°C)

  c. When instead a small amount of 40°C water is added, the temperature of the mixture will be

    (20°C) (between 20°C and 30°C) (30°C) (more than 30°C)

4. A red-hot piece of iron is put into a bucket of cool water. *Mark the following statements true (T) or false (F). (Ignore heat transfer to the bucket.)*

  a. The decrease in iron temperature equals the increase in the water temperature. ____F____   not same mass and heat capacity

  b. The quantity of heat lost by the iron equals the quantity of heat gained by the water. ____T____

  c. The iron and water both will reach the same temperature. ____T____

  d. The final temperature of the iron and water is halfway between the initial temperatures of each. ____F____

CAN COMMON ICE BE COLDER THAN 0°C?

Conceptual **PHYSICS**

5. The Computational Example on page 312 of your textbook shows the technique of unit conversion, called *dimensional analysis,* which indicates whether to multiply or divide when converting one quantity to another. The example converts Calories per day to watts. The *conversion factors* used in the example are (1 day)/(24 hour), (1 hour)/(3600 seconds), and (4184 joules)/(Calorie). The calorie here is the "big" calorie, commonly used in rating foods. Note carefully how the units cancel just as numbers do when multiplying fractions.

We will use this technique to solve the following: How many joules of energy are transferred per day at the rate of 1 watt? We know that 1 W is equal to 1 J/s. So

$$\frac{1 \text{ J}}{1 \text{ s}} \times \frac{3600 \text{ s}}{1 \text{ h}} \times \frac{24 \text{ h}}{1 \text{ d}} = \underline{\hspace{2cm}} \text{ J/d}$$

Note that in this case that (1 J)/(1 s) is multiplied by (3600 s)/(1 h) rather than by (1 h)/(3600 s). This way, the units s cancel. The same is true for units h. So 1 J is multiplied by 3600, since there are 3600 seconds in 1 hour, and again by 24, because there are 24 hours in 1 day. These numbers appear only in the numerators, so they are simply multiplied. We multiply the numerators and divide by the denominators. In this case we see only the numerical values of 1 appear in the demoninators.

a. By *dimensional analysis* convert 50 calories per hour (*small* calories) to joules per day.

$$\frac{50 \text{ cal}}{1 \text{ h}} \times \frac{\text{h}}{\text{d}} \times \frac{\text{J}}{\text{cal}} = \underline{\hspace{1.5cm}}$$

b. Try this one: How many joules will a 100-watt bulb give off in 4 hours?

$$100 \text{ W} \times 4 \text{ h} = \frac{\text{J}}{\text{s}} \times 4 \text{ h} \times \frac{\text{s}}{\text{h}} = \underline{\hspace{2cm}} \text{ J}$$

c. This one puts you more on your own: Find the number of calories given off by a 4-W bulb in a night light that burns continously for one month (1 mo).

$$4 \text{ W} \times 1 \text{ mo} = \frac{4 \text{ J}}{1 \text{ s}} \times 1 \text{ mo} \times \underline{\hspace{3cm}} = \underline{\hspace{2cm}} \text{ J}$$

6. On a certain planet the unit of heat energy is called the OOH, where 1 OOH = 3 calories, and the unit of time is called the AAH, where 1 AAH = 12.56 seconds. By *dimensional analysis* show that 1 watt = 1 OOH/AAH.

**Concept-Development
Practice Page** | **21-2**

Thermal Expansion

1. Long steel bridges often have one end fixed while the other end rests on rockers, as shown. Each sketch shows the bridge at a different season of the year. Mark the sketches winter (W) or summer (S). Briefly defend your answer.

( )   ( )

2. The weight hangs above the floor from the copper wire. When a candle is moved along the wire and heats it, what happens to the height of the weight above the floor? Why?

3. A steel television broadcasting tower is taller in the daytime than it is in the cooler nighttime. This is because steel expands (or contracts) about 1 part in 100 000 for each degree Celsius change. By this we mean that a piece of steel 100 000 units long will be 100 001 units long when its temperature increases by 1°C. What is the change in height for a 500-m steel tower when its temperature changes 20°C from day to night?

_____ cm

Conceptual PHYSICS

4. A common saying is "water seeks its own level," and usually it does. Here we see a container of water that is cooled on the left and warmed on the right. Consider the effect of temperature on density. Compared to the water level in the right tube, the water level in the left tube is

(slightly higher) (slightly lower) (the same)

5. The levels of water at 0°C and 1°C are shown below in the first two flasks. At these temperatures there is microscopic slush in the water. There is slightly more slush at 0°C than at 1°C. As the water is heated, some of the slush collapses as it melts, and the level of the water falls in the tube. That's why the level of water is slightly lower in the 1°C-tube. Make rough estimates and sketch in the appropriate levels of water at the other temperatures shown. What is important about the level when the water reaches 4°C?

6. The diagram at right shows an ice-covered pond. Mark the probable temperatures of water at the top and bottom of the pond.

I CAN'T GET THIS METAL LID OFF THE JAR... SHOULD I HEAT THE LID OR COOL IT? WHY? _____

WHICH WILL WEIGH MORE, 1 LITER OF ICE OR 1 LITER OF WATER?

Conceptual **PHYSICS**

Transmission of Heat

1. The tips of both brass rods are held in the gas flame.
   Mark the following true (T) or false (F).

   a. Heat is conducted only along Rod A._____

   b. Heat is conducted only along Rod B._____

   c. Heat is conducted equally along both

   Rod A and Rod B._____

   d. The idea that "heat rises" applies to heat transfer by *convection*, not by *conduction*.

   _____

2. Why does a bird fluff its feathers to keep warm on a cold day?

   _____

3. Why does a down-filled sleeping bag keep you warm on a cold night? Why is it useless if the down
   is wet?

   _____

4. What does *convection* have to do with the holes in the shade of the desk lamp?

   _____

5. The warmth of equatorial regions and coldness of polar
   regions on the earth can be understood by considering
   light from a flashlight striking a surface. If it strikes per-
   pendicularly, light energy is more concentrated as it
   covers a smaller area; if it strikes at an angle, the energy
   spreads over a larger area. So the energy per unit area is
   less.

   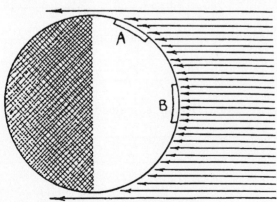

   The arrows represent rays of light from the
   distant sun incident upon the earth. Two
   areas of equal size are shown, Area A near the
   north pole and Area B near the equator.
   Count the rays that reach each area, and
   explain why B is warmer than A.

   _____

   _____

Conceptual **PHYSICS**

6. The earth's seasons result from the 23.5-degree tilt of the earth's daily spin axis as it orbits the sun. When the earth is at the point shown on the right in the sketch below (not to scale), the Northern Hemisphere tilts toward the sun, and sunlight striking it is strong (more rays per area). Sunlight striking the Southern Hemisphere is weak (fewer rays per area). Days in the north are warmer, and daylight is longer. You can see this by imagining the earth making its complete daily 24-hour spin.

Do two things on the sketch: (1) Shade the part of the earth in nighttime darkness for all positions, as is already done in the left position. (2) Label each position with the proper month — March, June, September, or December.

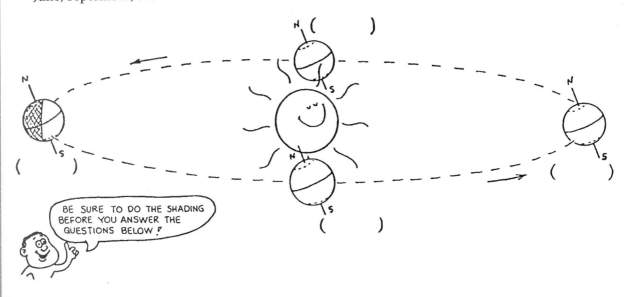

BE SURE TO DO THE SHADING BEFORE YOU ANSWER THE QUESTIONS BELOW !

a. When the earth is in any of the four positions shown, during one 24-hour spin a location at the equator receives sunlight half the time and is in darkness the other half the time.

   This means that regions at the equator always get about _____ hours of sunlight and

   _____ hours of darkness.

b. Can you see that in the June position regions farther north have longer daylight hours and shorter nights? Locations north of the Arctic Circle (dotted line in Northern Hemisphere) always face toward the sun as the earth spins, so they get daylight _____ hours a day.

c. How many hours of light and darkness are there in June at regions south of the Antarctic Circle (dotted line in Southern Hemisphere)?

   _____

d. Six months later, when the earth is at the December position, is the situation in the Antarctic the same or is it the reverse?

   _____

e. Why do South America and Australia enjoy warm weather in December instead of June?

   _____

   _____

Concept-Development Practice Page 23-1

Change of Phase

All matter can exist in the solid, liquid, or gaseous phases. The solid phase exists at relatively low temperatures, the liquid phase at higher temperatures, and the gaseous phase at still higher temperatures. Water is the most common example, not only because of its abundance but also because the temperatures for all three phases are common. Study Section 23.8 in your textbook and then answer the following:

1. How many calories are needed to change 1 gram of 0°C ice to water?

   _____

2. How many calories are needed to change the temperature of 1 gram of water by 1°C?

   _____

3. How many calories are needed to melt 1 gram of 0°C ice and turn it to water at a room temperature of 23°C?

   _____

4. A 50-gram sample of ice at 0°C is placed in a glass beaker that contains 200 g of water at 20°C.

   a. How much heat is needed to melt the ice? _____

   b. By how much would the temperature of the water change if it gave up this much heat to the ice? _____

   c. What will be the final temperature of the mixture? (Disregard any heat absorbed by the glass or given off by the surrounding air.) _____

5. How many calories are needed to change 1 gram of 100°C boiling water to 100°C steam?

   _____

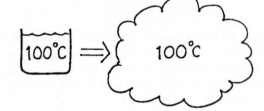

6. Fill in the number of calories at each step below for changing the state of 1 gram of 0°C ice to 100°C steam.

HEAT NEEDED = _____ CAL + _____ CAL + _____ CAL = _____ CAL

Conceptual PHYSICS

7. One gram of steam at 100°C condneses, and the water cools to 22°C.

    a. How much heat is released when the steam condenses?_____

    b. How much heat is released when the water cools from 100°C to 22°C?

    _____

    c. How much heat is released altogether? _____

8. In a household radiator 1000 g of steam at 100°C condenses, and the water cools to 90°C.

    a. How much heat is released when the steam condenses?

    _____

    b. How much heat is released when the water cools from 100°C to 90°C?

    _____

    c. How much heat is released altogether?

    _____

9. Why is it difficult to make tea on the top of a high mountain?

    _____

10. How many calories are given up by 1 gram of 100°C steam that condenses to 100°C water?

    _____

11. How many calories are given up by 1 gram of 100°C steam that condenses and drops in temperature to 22°C water?

    _____

12. How many calories are given to a household radiator when 1000 grams of 100°C steam condenses, and drops in temperature to 90°C water?

    _____

13. To get water from the ground, even in the hot desert, dig a hole about a half meter wide and a half meter deep. Place a cup at the bottom. Spread a sheet of plastic wrap over the hole and place stones along the edge to hold it secure. Weight the center of the plastic with a stone so it forms a cone shape. Why will water collect in the cup? (Physics can save your life if you're ever stranded in a desert!)

_____

_____

_____

_____

_____

_____

Conceptual **PHYSICS**

Evaporation

1. Why does it feel colder when you swim at a pool on a windy day?

   _____

2. Why does your skin feel cold when a little rubbing alcohol is applied to it?

   _____

3. Briefly explain from a molecular point of view why evaporation is a cooling process.

   _____

   _____

4. When hot water rapidly evaporates, the result can be dramatic. Consider 4 g of boiling water spread over a large surface so that 1 g rapidly evaporates. Suppose further that the surface and surroundings are very cold so that all 540 calories for evaporation come from the remaining 3 g of water.

   a. How many calories are taken from each gram of water?

   _____

   b. How many calories are released when 1 g of 100°C water cools to 0°C?

   _____

   c. How many calories are released when 1 g of 0°C water changes to 0°C ice?

   _____

   d. What happens in this case to the remaining 3 g of boiling water when 1 g rapidly evaporates?

   _____

   _____

Conceptual PHYSICS

**Concept-Development
Practice Page**

24-1

Thermodynamics

A mass of air is contained so that the volume can change but the pressure remains constant. Table I shows air volumes at various temperatures when the air is heated slowly.

1. Plot the data in Table I on the graph, and connect the points.

Table I

TEMP. (°C)	VOLUME (mL)
0	50
25	55
50	60
75	65
100	70

VOLUME (mL)

70
60
50
40
30
20
10

-200   -100   0   50   100

TEMPERATURE (°C)

2. The graph shows how the volume of air varies with temperature at constant pressure. The straightness of the line means that the air expands uniformly with temperature. From your graph, you can predict what will happen to the volume of air when it is cooled.

   Extrapolate (extend) the straight line of your graph to find the temperature at which the volume of the air would become zero. Mark this point on your graph. Estimate this

   temperature: _____

3. Although air would liquify before cooling to this temperature, the procedure suggests that there is a lower limit to how cold something can be. This is the absolute zero of temperature.

   Careful experiments show that absolute zero is _____ °C.

4. Scientists measure temperature in *kelvins* instead of degrees Celsius, where the absolute zero of temperature is 0 kelvins. If you relabeled the temperature axis on the graph in Question 1 so that it

   shows temperature in kelvins, would your graph look like the one below? _____

VOLUME (mL)

70
60
50
40
30
20
10

0   273   373

TEMPERATURE (K)

Conceptual **PHYSICS**

Chapter 24 Thermodynamics   **87**

Vibrations and Waves

1. A sine curve that represents a transverse wave is drawn below. With a ruler, measure the wavelength and amplitude of the wave.

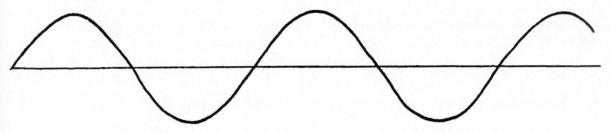

    a.   Wavelength = _____   b. Amplitude = _____

2. A kid on a playground swing makes a complete to-and-fro swing each 2 seconds. The frequency of swing is

      (0.5 hertz)   (1 hertz)   (2 hertz)

   and the period is

      (0.5 second)   (1 second)   (2 seconds)

3. *Complete the statements.*

THE PERIOD OF A 440-HERTZ SOUND WAVE IS _____ SECOND.

A MARINE WEATHER STATION REPORTS WAVES ALONG THE SHORE THAT ARE 8 SECONDS APART. THE FREQUENCY OF THE WAVES IS THEREFORE _____ HERTZ.

4. The annoying sound from a mosquito is produced when it beats its wings at the average rate of 600 wingbeats per second.

   a. What is the frequency of the soundwaves?

     _____

   b. What is the wavelength? (Assume the speed of sound is 340 m/s.)

     _____

Conceptual **PHYSICS**

5. A machine gun fires 10 rounds per second.
   The speed of the bullets is 300 m/s.

   a. What is the distance in the air between the flying bullets?_____

   b. What happens to the distance between the bullets if the rate of fire is increased?

   _____

6. Consider a wave generator that produces 10 pulses per second. The speed of the waves is
   300 cm/s.

   a. What is the wavelength of the waves? _____

   b. What happens to the wavelength if the frequency of pulses is increased?

   _____

7. The bird at the right watches the waves. If the portion of a wave between 2 crests passes the pole
   each second, what is the speed of the wave?

   _____

   What is its period?

   _____

8. If the distance between crests in the
   above question were 1.5 meters apart,
   and 2 crests pass the pole each second,
   what would be the speed of the wave?

   _____

   What would be its period?

   _____

9. When an automobile moves toward a
   listener, the sound of its horn seems
   relatively

   (low pitched)   (normal)

   (high pitched)

   and when moving away from the listener,
   its horn seems

   (low pitched)   (normal)

   (high pitched)

10. The changed pitch of the Doppler effect is due to changes in

   (wave speed)   (wave frequency)

Conceptual **PHYSICS**

Shock Waves

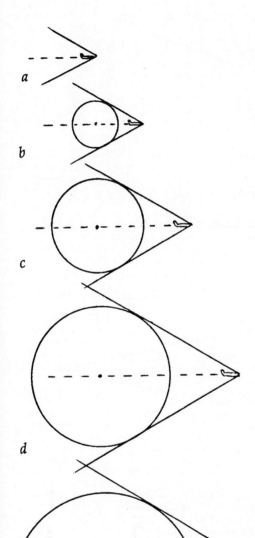

The cone-shaped shock wave produced by a supersonic aircraft is actually the result of overlapping spherical waves of sound, as shown in Figure 25·22 in your textbook. Sketches *a, b, c, d,* and *e,* at the left show the "animated" growth of only one of the many spherical sound waves (shown as an expanding circle in the two-dimensional sketch). The circle originates when the aircraft is in the position shown in *a.* Sketch *b* shows both the growth of the circle and position of the aircraft at a later time. Still later times are shown in *c, d,* and *e.* Note that the circle grows and the aircraft moves farther to the right. Note also that the aircraft is moving farther than the sound wave. This is because the aircraft is moving faster than sound.

Careful examination will reveal how fast the aircraft is moving compared to the speed of sound. Sketch *e* shows that in the same time the sound travels from O to A, the aircraft has traveled from O to B — twice as far. You can check this with a ruler.

Circle the answer.

1. Inspect sketches *b* and *d*. Has the aircraft traveled twice as far as sound in the same time in these postions also?

    (yes)   (no)

2. For greater speeds, the angle of the shock wave would be

    (wider)   (the same)   (narrower)

> DURING THE TIME THAT SOUND TRAVELS FROM O TO A, THE PLANE TRAVELS TWICE AS FAR --- FROM O TO B.

> SO IT'S FLYING AT TWICE THE SPEED OF SOUND !

3. Use a ruler to estimate the speeds of the aircraft that produce the shock waves in the two sketches below.

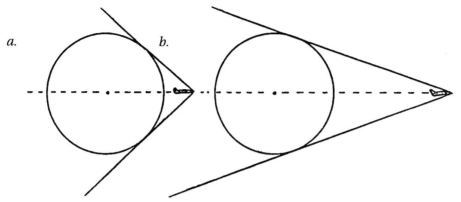

Aircraft *a* is traveling about _____ times the speed of sound.

Aircraft *b* is traveling about _____ times the speed of sound.

4. Draw your own circle (anywhere) and estimate the speed of the aircraft to produce the shock wave shown below.

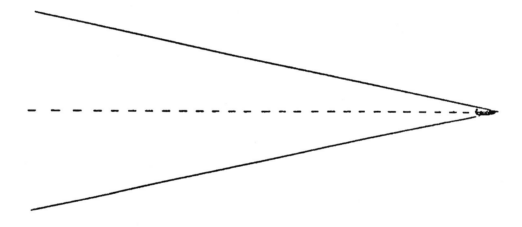

The speed is about _____ times the speed of sound.

5. In the space below, draw the shock wave made by a supersonic missile that travels at four times the speed of sound.

Conceptual **PHYSICS**

Concept-Development Practice Page 25-3

Wave Superposition

A pair of pulses travel toward each at equal speeds. The composite waveforms as they pass through each other and interfere are shown at 1-second intervals. In the left column note how the pulses interfere to produce the composite waveform (solid line). Make a similar construction for the two wave pulses in the right column. Like the pulses in the first column, they each travel at 1 space per second.

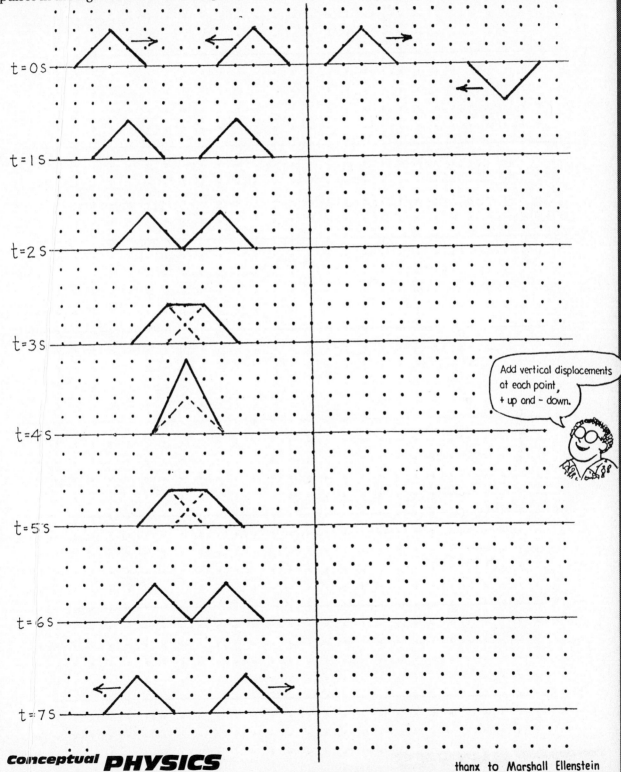

Add vertical displacements at each point, + up and – down.

Conceptual PHYSICS

thanx to Marshall Ellenstein

Construct the composite waveforms at 1-second intervals for the two waves traveling toward each other at equal speed.

$t = 0\,s$

$t = 1\,s$

$t = 2\,s$

$t = 3\,s$

$t = 4\,s$

$t = 5\,s$

$t = 6\,s$

$t = 7\,s$

$t = 8\,s$

Sound

1. Two major classes of waves are *longitudinal* and *transverse*. Sound waves are

     (longitudinal)   (transverse)

2. The frequency of a sound signal refers to how frequently the vibrations occur. A high-frequency sound is heard at a high

     (pitch)   (wavelength)   (speed)

3. The sketch below shows a snap shot of the compressions and rarefactions of the air in a tube as the sound moves toward the right. The dots represent molecules. With a ruler the wavelength of the sound wave is measured to be _____ cm.

4. Compared to the wavelengths of high-pitched sounds, the wavelengths of low-pitched sounds are

     (long)   (short)

5. Suppose you set your watch by the sound of the noon whistle from a factory 3 km away.

   a. Compared to the correct time, your watch will be
      (behind)   (ahead)

   b. It will differ from the correct time by
      (3 seconds)   (6 seconds)   (9 seconds)

Conceptual **PHYSICS**

6. Sound waves travel fastest in

   (solids) (liquids) (gases)

   (...same speed in each)

7. If the child's natural frequency of swinging is once each 4 seconds, for maximum amplitude the man should push at a rate of once each

   (2 seconds) (4 seconds) (8 seconds)

8. If the man in Question 7 pushes in the same direction twice as often, his pushes

   (will) (will not)

   be effective because

   (the swing will be pushed twice as often in the right direction)

   (every other push will oppose the motion of the swing)

9. The frequency of the tuning fork is 440 hertz. It will NOT be forced into vibration by a sound of

   (220 hertz) (440 hertz) (880 hertz)

10. Beats are the result of the alternate cancellation and reinforcement of two sound waves of

    (the same frequency) (slightly different frequencies)

11. Two notes with frequencies of 66 and 70 Hz are sounded together. The resulting beat frequency is

    (4 hertz) (68 hertz) (136 hertz)

12. The accepted value for the speed of sound in air is 332 m/s at 0°C. The speed of sound in air increases 0.6 m/s for each Celsius degree above zero. Compute the speed of sound at the temperature of the room you are now in.

Concept-Development Practice Page   **27-1**

Light

1. The Danish astronomer Olaus Roemer made careful measurements of the period of a moon about the planet Jupiter. How this data enabled a calculation of the speed of light is described in your textbook on pages 405 and 406.

   a. What is the diameter, in kilometers, of the earth's orbit around the sun?

     _____

   b. How much time is required for light to travel across the diameter of the orbit?

     _____

   c. How do these two quantities determine the speed of light?

     _____

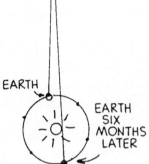

2. Study Figure 27.4 on page 408 in your textbook and answer the following:

   a. Which has the longer *wavelengths*, radio waves or light waves?

     _____

   b. Which has the longer *wavelengths*, light waves or gamma rays?

     _____

   c. Which has the higher *frequencies*, ultraviolet or infrared waves?

     _____

   d. Which has the higher *frequencies*, ultraviolet waves or gamma rays?

     _____

3. Carefully study Section 27.4 in your textbook and answer the following:

   a. Exactly what do vibrating electrons emit?

     _____

   b. When ultraviolet light shines on glass, what does it do to electrons in the glass structure?

     _____

   c. When energetic electrons in the glass structure vibrate against neighboring atoms, what happens to the energy of vibration?

     _____

   d. What happens to the energy of a vibrating electron that does not collide with neighboring atoms?

     _____

Conceptual **PHYSICS**

e. Which range of light frequencies, visible or ultraviolet, are absorbed in glass?

_____

f. Which range of light frequencies, visible or ultraviolet, are transmitted through glass?

_____

g. How is the speed of light in glass affected by the succession of time delays that accompany the absorption and re-emission of light from atom to atom in the glass?

_____

h. How does the speed of light compare in water, glass, and diamond?

_____

4. The sun normally shines on both the earth and on the moon. Both cast shadows. Sometimes the moon's shadow falls on the earth, and at other times the earth's shadow falls on the moon.

a. The sketch shows the sun and the earth. Draw the moon at a position for a solar eclipse.

b. This sketch also shows the sun and the earth. Draw the moon at a position for a lunar eclipse.

5. The diagram shows the limits of light rays when a large lamp makes a shadow of a small object on a screen. Shade the umbra darker than the penumbra. In what part of the shadow could an ant see part of the lamp?

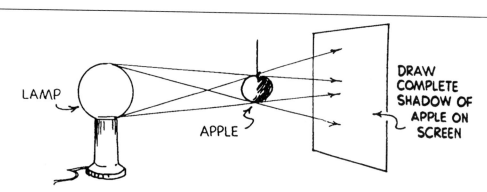

Conceptual **PHYSICS**

Polarization

The amplitude of a light wave has magnitude and direction, and can be represented by a vector. Polarized light vibrates in a single direction and is represented by a single vector. To the left the single vector represents vertically polarized light. The vibrations of non-polarized light are equal in all directions. There are as many vertical components as horizontal components. The pair of perpendicular vectors to the right represents non-polarized light.

1. In the sketch below non-polarized light from a flashlight strikes a pair of Polaroid filters.

NON-POLARIZED LIGHT VIBRATES IN ALL DIRECTIONS
HORIZONTAL AND VERTICAL COMPONENTS
VERTICAL COMPONENT PASSES THROUGH FIRST POLARIZER
...AND THE SECOND

VERTICAL COMPONENT DOES NOT PASS THROUGH THIS SECOND POLARIZER

a. Light is transmitted by a pair of Polaroids when their axes are

   (aligned)   (crossed at right angles)

   and light is blocked when their axes are

   (aligned)   (crossed at right angles)

b. Transmitted light is polarized in a direction

   (the same as)   (different than)   the polarization axis of the filter.

2. Consider the transmission of light through a pair of Polaroids with polarization axes at 45° to each other. Although in practice the Polaroids are one atop the other, we show them spread out side by side below. From left to right: (*a*) Nonpolarized light is represented by its horizontal and vertical components. (*b*) These components strike filter A. (*c*) The vertical component is transmitted, and (*d*) falls upon filter B. This vertical component is not aligned with the polarization axis of filter B, but it has a component that is — component *t*; (*e*) which is transmitted.

(a)   A   (b)   (c)   B   (d)   (e)

a. The amount of light that gets through Filter B, compared to the amount that gets through Filter A is

   (more)   (less)   (the same)

b. The component perpendicular to *t* that falls on Filter B is

   (also transmitted)   (absorbed)

Conceptual **PHYSICS**

3. Below are a pair of Polaroids with polarization axes at 30° to each other. Carefully draw vectors and appropriate components (as in Question 2) to show the vector that emerges at *e*.

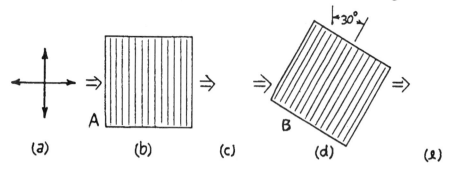

(a)   (b)   (c)   (d)   (e)

    a. The amount of light that gets through the Polaroids at 30°, compared to the amount that gets though the 45° Polaroids is

      (less)   (more)   (the same)

4. Figure 27.19 in your textbook shows the smile of Ludmila Hewitt emerging through three Polaroids. Use vector diagrams to complete steps *b* through *g* below to show how light gets through the three-Polaroid system.

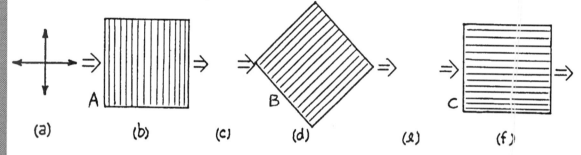

(a)   (b)   (c)   (d)   (e)   (f)

5. A novel use of polarization is shown below. How do the polarized side windows in these next-to-each-other houses provide privacy for the occupants? (Who can see what?)

SIDE WINDOWS POLARIZED GLASS

_____

_____

_____

Color

1. The sketch shows the shadow of your hand held in front of a white screen in a darkened room. The light source is red, so the screen looks red and the shadow looks black. Color the sketch with colored markers, or label the colors with pen or pencil.

2. A green lamp is turned on and makes a second shadow. The formerly black shadow cast by the red light is no longer black, but is illuminated with green light. So it is green. Color or mark it green. The shadow cast by the green lamp is not black, because it is illuminated with the red light. Color or mark its color. The background receives a mixture of red and green light. Figure out what color the background will appear, then color or label it.

3. A blue lamp is turned on and three shadows of your hand appear. Color or label the appropriate colors of the shadows and the background.

4. If you have colored markers, have a go at these.

Reflection

1. Light from a flashlight shines on a mirror and illuminates one of the cards. Draw the reflected beam to indicate the illuminated card.

2. A periscope has a pair of mirrors in it. Draw the light path from the object "O" to the eye of the observer.

3. The ray diagram below shows the extension of one of the reflected rays from the plane mirror. Complete the diagram by (1) carefully drawing the three other reflected rays, and (2) extending them behind the mirror to locate the image of the flame. (Assume the candle and image are viewed by an observer on the left.)

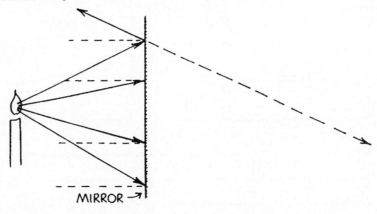

4. The ray diagram below shows the reflection of one of the rays that strikes the parabolic mirror. Notice that the law of reflection is obeyed, and the angle of incidence (from the normal, the dashed line) equals the angle of reflection (from the normal). Complete the diagram by drawing the reflected rays of the other three rays that are shown. (Do you see why parabolic mirrors are used in automobile headlights?)

MIRROR

5. A girl takes a photograph of the bridge as shown. Which of the two sketches correctly shows the reflected view of the bridge? Defend your answer.

_____

_____

_____

_____

Conceptual **PHYSICS**

Name _____ Period _____ Date _____

Reflection

MIRROR

ABE BEV

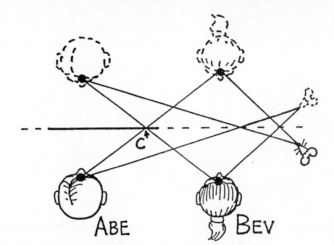

ABE BEV

Abe and Bev both look in a plane mirror directly in front of Abe (left, top view). Abe can see himself while Bev cannot see herself—but can Abe see Bev, and can Bev see Abe? To find the answer we construct their artificial locations "through" the mirror, the same distance behind as Abe and Bev are in front (right, top view). If straight-line connections intersect the mirror, as at point C, then each sees the other. The mouse, for example, cannot see or be seen by Abe and Bev.

Here we have eight students in front of a small plane mirror. Their positions are shown in the diagram below. Make appropriate straight-line constructions to answer the following:

MIRROR

ABE BEV CIS DON EVA FLO GUY HAN

Who can Abe see? _____ Who can Abe not see? _____
Who can Bev see? _____ Who can Bev not see? _____
Who can Cis see? _____ Who can Cis not see? _____
Who can Don see? _____ Who can Don not see? _____
Who can Eva see? _____ Who can Eva not see? _____
Who can Flo see? _____ Who can Flo not see? _____
Who can Guy see? _____ Who can Guy not see? _____
Who can Han see? _____ Who can Han not see? _____

Conceptual **PHYSICS**

thanx to Marshall Ellenstein

Chapter 29 Reflection and Refraction

Six of our group are now arranged differently in front of the same mirror. Their positions are shown below. Make appropriate constructions for this more interesting arrangement, and answer the questions below.

ABE

EVA

BEV

FLO

CIS

DON

Who can Abe see? _____ Who can Abe not see? _____
Who can Bev see? _____ Who can Bev not see? _____
Who can Cis see? _____ Who can Cis not see? _____
Who can Don see? _____ Who can Don not see? _____
Who can Eva see? _____ Who can Eva not see? _____
Who can Flo see? _____ Who can Flo not see? _____

Harry Hotshot views himself in a full-length mirror (right). Construct straight lines from Harry's eyes to the image of his feet, and to the top of his head. Mark the mirror to indicate the minimum area Harry uses to see a full view of himself.

Does this region of the mirror depend on Harry's distance from the mirror?

Refraction

1. A pair of toy cart wheels are rolled obliquely from a smooth surface onto two plots of grass —
   a rectangular plot as shown at the left, and a triangular plot as shown at the right. The ground is
   on a slight incline so that after slowing down in the grass, the wheels speed up again when
   emerging on the smooth surface. Finish each sketch and show some positions of the wheels
   inside the plots and on the other side. Clearly indicate their paths and directions of travel.

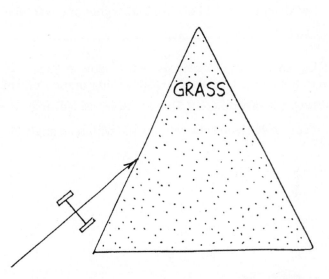

2. Red, green, and blue rays of light are incident upon a glass prism as shown. The average speed of
   red light in the glass is less than in air, so the red ray is refracted. When it emerges into the air it
   regains its original speed and travels in the direction shown. Green light takes longer to get
   through the glass. Because of its slower speed it is refracted as shown. Blue light travels even
   slower in glass. Complete the diagram by estimating the path of the blue ray.

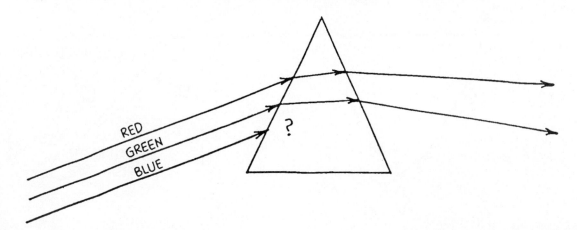

Conceptual PHYSICS

3. The sketch shows that due to refraction, the man sees the fish closer to the water surface than it actually is.

   a. Draw a ray beginning at the fish's eye to show the line of sight of the fish when it looks upward at 50° to the normal at the water surface. Draw the direction of the ray after it meets the surface of the water and continues in the air.

   b. At the 50° angle, does the fish see the man, or does it see the reflected view of the starfish at the bottom of the pond? Explain.

   _____

   _____

   c. To see the man, should the fish look higher or lower than the 50° path?

   _____

   d. If the fish's eye were barely above the water surface, it would see the world above in a 180° view, horizon to horizon. The fisheye view of the world above as seen beneath the water, however, is very different. Due to the 48° critical angle of water, the fish sees a normally 180° horizon-to-horizon view compressed within an angle of _____.

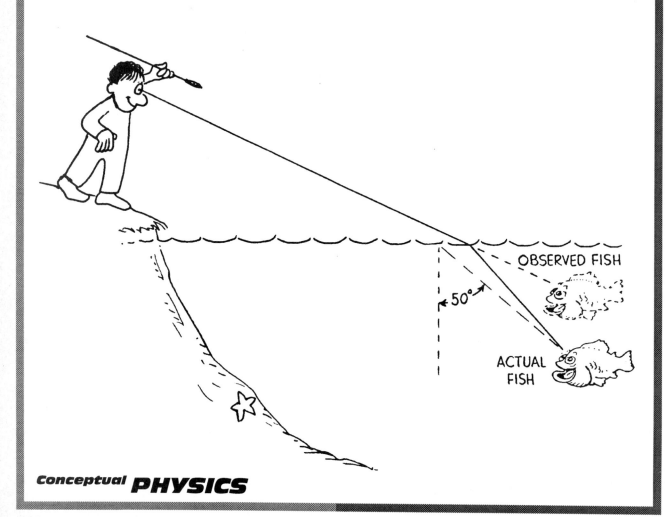

Conceptual **PHYSICS**

Refraction

1. The sketch to the right shows a light ray moving from air into water, at 45° to the normal. Which of the three rays indicated with capital letters is most likely the light ray that continues inside the water?

_____

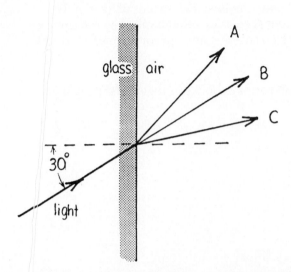

2. The sketch on the left shows a light ray moving from glass into air, at 30° to the normal. Which of the three is most likely the light ray that continues in the air?

_____

3. To the right, a light ray is shown moving from air into a glass block, at 40° to the normal. Which of the three rays is most likely the light ray that travels in the air after emerging from the opposite side of the block?

_____

Sketch the path the light would take inside the glass.

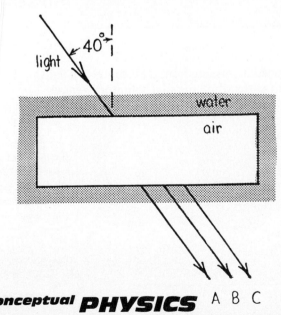

4. To the left, a light ray is shown moving from water into a rectangular block of air (inside a thin-walled plastic box), at 40° to the normal. Which of the three rays is most likely the light ray that continues into the water on the opposite side of the block?

_____

Sketch the path the light would take inside the air.

Conceptual PHYSICS   A B C

thanx to Clarence Bakken

5. The two transparent blocks (right) are made of different materials. The speed of light in the left block is greater than the speed of light in the right block. Draw an appropriate light path through and beyond the right block. Is the light that emerges displaced more or less than light emerging from the left block?

_____

6. Light from the air passes through plates of glass and plastic below. The speeds of light in the different materials is shown to the right (these different speeds are often implied by the "index of refraction" of the material). Construct a rough sketch showing an appropriate path through the system of four plates.

Compared to the 50° incident ray at the top, what can you say about the angles of the ray in the air between and below the block pairs?

_____

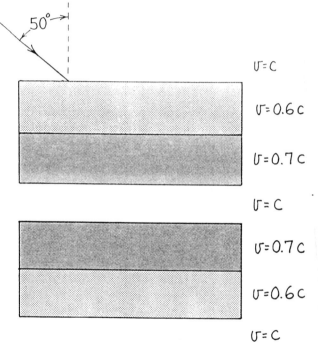

7. Parallel rays of light are refracted as they change speed in passing from air into the eye (left). Construct a rough sketch showing appropriate light paths when parallel light under water meets the same eye (right).

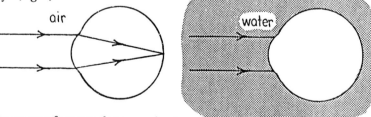

If a fish out of water wishes to clearly view objects in air, should it wear goggles filled with water or with air?

8. Why do we need to wear a face mask or goggles to see clearly when under water?

_____

Pinhole Image Formation

Look carefully at the round spots of light on the shady ground beneath trees. These are sunballs, and are actually images of the sun. They are cast by openings between leaves in the trees that act as pinholes (see Activity 1 at the end of Chapter 30 in your textbook). Large sunballs, several centimeters in diameter or so, are cast by openings that are relatively high above the ground, while small ones are pro-

duced by closer "pinholes." The interesting point is that the ratio of the diameter of the sunball to its distance from the pinhole is the same as the ratio of the sun's diameter to its distance from the pinhole. We know the sun is approximately 150 000 000 km from the pinhole, so careful measurement of this ratio tells us the diameter of the sun. That's what this page is about. Instead of finding sunballs under the shade of trees, make your own easier-to-measure sunballs.

150,000,000 km

1. Poke a small hole in a piece of cardboard (like with a sharp pencil). Hold the cardboard in the sunlight and note the circular image that is cast. This is an image of the sun. Note that its size does not depend on the size of the hole in the cardboard, but only on its distance. The image will be a circle when cast on a surface that is perpendicular to the rays — otherwise it will be "stretched out" as an ellipse.

2. If you were doing this when the sun is partially eclipsed, what image shape would you

    expect to see? _____

3. Try holes of different shapes — say a square hole, or a triangular hole. What is the shape of the image when its distance from the cardboard is large compared to the size of the hole?

    _____ Does the shape of the "pinhole" make a difference? _____

4. Measure the diameter of a small coin. Then place the coin on a viewing area that is perpendicular to the sun's rays. Position the cardboard so the image exactly covers the coin. Carefully measure the distance between the coin and the the small hole in the cardboard. Complete the following:

WHAT SHAPE DO SUNBALLS HAVE DURING A PARTIAL ECLIPSE OF THE SUN ?

$$\frac{\text{Diameter of sunball}}{\text{Distance to pinhole}} = \underline{\qquad}$$

With this ratio, estimate the diameter of the sun. Show your work on the back.

Conceptual PHYSICS

**Concept-Development
Practice Page**   **30-2**

Lenses

Rays of light bend as shown when passing through the glass blocks.

1. Show how light rays bend when they pass through the arrangement of glass blocks shown below.

2. Show how light rays bend when they pass through the lens shown below. Is the lens a converging or a diverging lens? What is your evidence?

_____

_____

3. Show how light rays bend when they pass through the arrangement of glass blocks shown below.

4. Show how light rays bend when they pass through the lens shown below. Is the lens a converging or a diverging lens? What is your evidence?

_____

_____

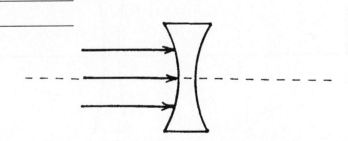

Conceptual PHYSICS

5. Which type of lens is used to correct farsightedness? _____ _____

   Nearsightedness? _____ _____

6. Use the ray-diagram technique (described in Section 30.3 of your text) to find the location and relative size of the arrow's image for each of the lenses below.

Concept-Development Practice Page 31-1

Diffraction and Interference

1. Shown below are concentric solid and dashed circles, each different in radius by 1 cm. Consider the circular pattern a top view of water waves, where the solid circles are crests and the dashed circles are troughs.

   a. Draw another set of the same concentric circles with a compass. Choose any part of the paper for your center (except the present central point). Let the circles run off the edge of the paper.

   b. Find where a dashed line crosses a solid line and draw a large dot at the intersection. Do this for ALL places where a solid and dashed line intersect.

   c. With a wide felt marker, connect the dots with smooth lines. These *nodal lines* lie in regions where the waves have cancelled — where the crest of one wave overlaps the trough of another (see Figures 25.11 and 31.12 in the textbook).

Conceptual PHYSICS

2. Look at the construction of overlapping circles on your classmates' papers. Some will have more nodal lines than others, due to different starting points. How does the number of nodal lines in a pattern relate to the distance between centers of circles, (or sources of waves)?

_____

_____

3. Figure 31.16 from your text is repeated below. Carefully count the number of wavelengths (same as the number of wave crests) along the following paths between the slits and the screen.

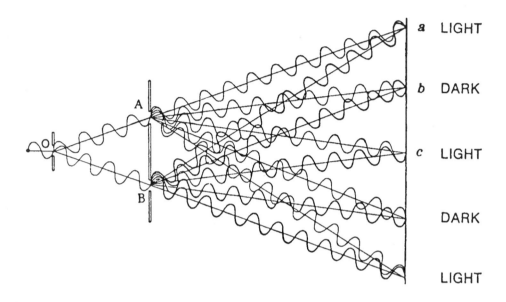

a. Number of wavelengths between slit A and point *a* = _____

b. Number of wavelengths between slit B and point *a* = _____

c. Number of wavelengths between slit A and point *b* = _____

d. Number of wavelengths between slit B and point *b* = _____

e. Number of wavelengths between slit A and point *c* = _____

f. Number of wave crests between slit B and point *c* = _____

When the number of wavelengths along each path is the same or differs by one or more whole wavelengths, interference is

(constructive) (destructive).

and when the number of wavelengths differ by a half wavelength (or odd multiples of a half wavelength), interference is

(constructive) (destructive).

Electric Field

1. An *electric field* surrounds an electric charge. The field strength at any place in the field can be found by placing a small positive test charge there. Where the force on the test charge is great, the field strength is great; where the force is weak, the field strength is weak. Electric field strength is directly proportional to the force exerted on a positive test charge.

    The direction of an electric field at any point is the same as the direction of the force exerted on the positive test charge.

    Some electric field lines surrounding a positive charge are shown above. They extend radially from the charge. A vector is sketched at point *a* to represent the force that would be exerted on a positive test charge there (its direction shows that like charges repel). Other points *b,c,d,e* and *f*, are all located at the same distance from the positive charge.

    Draw a vector at each point *b - f* to show the force on the same test charge.

2. The electric field about a negative charge is shown to the right. The field lines point radially inward, in the same direction a positive test charge would be forced. Assume the magnitude of the negative charge is the same as the charge above.

    Draw field vectors at each of the points *h - m*.

3. The pair of equal and opposite charges of Questions 1 and 2 is shown below. Their individual fields, drawn uninfluenced by each other, overlap to form a field pattern that can be constructed by vector rules. This is shown at locations *a* and *b*, where the two forces combine to a single resultant force. Note that point *b* overlaps point *m*, and also points *c* and *l* overlap. Note how the size of each vector depends on its distance from the charge (inverse-square law). Every point in the field is the result of both the positive and the negative charges.

    By vector rules, show the resultant of all the vector pairs shown. Then sketch in sample vector resultants at a few other places. Does the pattern that emerges agree with the field patterns shown in Figure a on the next page? _____

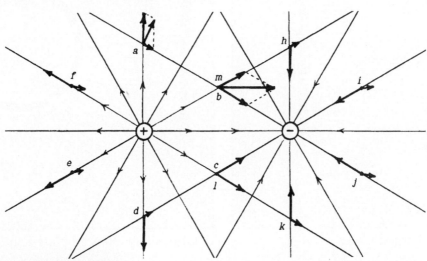

Conceptual PHYSICS

4. A copy of Figure 33.5 in your textbook is shown below. Three points, (*a, b, c*) are indicated on each electric field pattern. Point *a* in each pattern shows the electric field vector at that point. The vector indicates the magnitude and direction of the force that a positive test charge would experience at that point (a curved field indicates that the force on a nearby test charge would be different in magnitude and direction). Use the vector at points *a* as a reference and sketch in the electric field vectors for points *b* and *c* in each pattern, using colored ink or pencil.

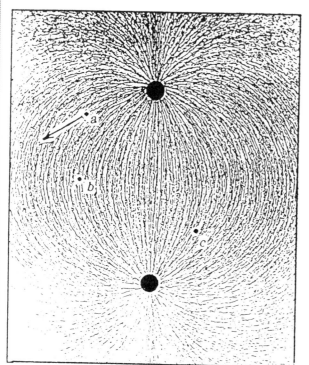

a. Equal and opposite charges

b. Equal like charges

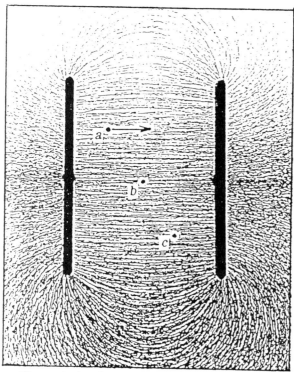

c. Oppositely charged plates

d. Oppositely charged plate and cylinder

Conceptual PHYSICS

Electric Potential

1.   Just as PE (potential energy) transforms to KE (kinetic energy) for a mass lifted against the gravitational field (left), the electric PE of an electric charge transforms to other forms of energy when it changes location in an electric field (right). When released, how does the KE acquired by each compare to the decrease in PE?

_____

2. *Complete the statements.*

A force compresses the spring. The work done in compression is the product of the average force and the distance moved. W = Fd. This work increases the PE of the spring.

Similarly, a force pushes the charge (call it a test charge) closer

to the charged sphere. The work done in moving the test charge

is the product of the average _____ and the _____ moved.

W = _____. This work _____ the PE of the test charge.

If the test charge is released, it will be repelled and fly past the starting point. Its gain in KE at this

point is _____ to its decrease in PE.

At any point, a greater quantity of test charge means a greater amount of PE, but not a greater amount of PE *per quantity* of charge. The quantities PE (measured in joules) and PE/charge (measured in volts) are different concepts.

By definition: **Electric Potential = PE/charge.** 1 volt = 1 joule/1coulomb.

3. *Complete the statements.*

ELECTRIC PE/CHARGE HAS THE SPECIAL NAME *ELECTRIC* _____

SINCE IT IS MEASURED IN *VOLTS* IT IS COMMONLY CALLED _____

Conceptual **PHYSICS**

4. When a charge of 1 C has an electric PE of 1 J, it has an electric potential of 1 V. When a charge of 2 C has an electric PE of 2 J, its potential is = _____ V.

5. If a conductor connected to the terminal of a battery has a potential of 12 volts, then each coulomb of charge on the conductor has a PE of _____ J.

6. If a charge of 1 C has a PE of 5000 J, its voltage is _____ V.

7. If a charge of 0.001 C has a PE of 5 J, its voltage is _____ V.

8. If a charge of 0.0001 C has a PE of 0.5 J, its voltage is _____ V.

9. If a rubber balloon is charged to 5000 V, and the quantity of charge on the balloon is 1 millionth coulomb, (0.000001 C) then the PE of this charge is only _____ J.

10. Some people get mixed up between force and pressure. Recall that pressure is force *per area*. Similarly, some people get mixed up between electric PE and voltage. According to this chapter, voltage is electric PE *per* _____.

ELECTRIC POTENTIAL IS NOT THE SAME AS ELECTRIC POTENTIAL ENERGY (PE). VOLTAGE AND ELECTRIC POTENTIAL ARE THE SAME. WE'LL SEE IN THE NEXT CHAPTER THEY ARE A SORT OF "ELECTRIC PRESSURE".

Electric Current

1. Water doesn't flow in the pipe when
(**a**) both ends are at the same level.
Another way of saying this is that water
will not flow in the pipe when both ends
have the same potential energy (PE).
Similarly, charge will not flow in a conductor
if both ends of the conductor are at the same
electric potential. But tip the water pipe and
increase the PE of one side so there is a difference
in PE across the ends of the pipe, as in (**b**), and water
will flow. Similarly, increase the electric potential of one
end of an electric conductor so there is a potential difference across the ends, and charge will
flow.

a. The units of electric potential difference are

(volts) (amperes) (ohms) (watts)

b. It is common to call electric potential difference

(voltage) (amperage) (wattage)

c. The flow of electric charge is called electric

(voltage) (current) (power),

and is measured in

(volts) (amperes) (ohms) (watts)

*A VOLT IS A UNIT OF _____
AND AN AMPERE IS A UNIT OF _____*

*DOES VOLTAGE CAUSE CURRENT,
OR DOES CURRENT CAUSE VOLTAGE?
WHICH IS THE CAUSE AND WHICH
IS THE EFFECT?*

2. Complete the statements:

a. A current of 1 ampere is a flow of charge at the rate of _____ coulomb per second.

b. When a charge of 15 C flows through any area in a circuit each second, the current is

_____ A.

c. One volt is the potential difference between two points if 1 joule of energy is needed to move

_____ coulomb of charge between the two points.

d. When a lamp is plugged into a 120-V socket, each coulomb of charge that flows in the circuit

is raised to a potential energy of _____ joules.

e. Which offers more resistance to water flow, a wide pipe or a narrow pipe? _____
Similarly, which offers more resistance to the flow of charge, a thick wire or a thin wire?

_____

Conceptual PHYSICS

Ohm's Law

1. How much current flows in a 1000-ohm resistor when 1.5 volts are impressed across it?

   _____

2. If the filament resistance in an automobile headlamp is 3 ohms, how many amps does it draw when connected to a 12-volt battery?

   _____

3. The resistance of the side lights on an automobile are 10 ohms. How much current flows in them when connected to 12 volts?

   _____

4. What is the current in the 30-ohm heating coil of a coffee maker that operates on a 120-volt circuit?

   _____

CURRENT = $\frac{VOLTAGE}{RESISTANCE}$ OR $I = \frac{V}{R}$

USE OHM'S LAW IN THE TRIANGLE TO FIND THE QUANTITY YOU WANT, COVER THE LETTER WITH YOUR FINGER AND THE REMAINING TWO SHOW YOU THE FORMULA !

$\frac{V}{I \times R}$

CONDUCTORS AND RESISTORS HAVE RESISTANCE TO THE CURRENT IN THEM.

5. During a lie detector test, a voltage of 6 V is impressed across two fingers. When a certain question is asked, the resistance between the fingers drops from 400 000 ohms to 200 000 ohms. What is the current (a) initially through the fingers, and (b) when the resistance between them drops?

   (a) _____ (b) _____

6. How much resistance allows an impressed voltage of 6 V to produce a current of 0.006 A?

   _____

7. What is the resistance of a clothes iron that draws a current of 12 A at 120 V?

   _____

OHM MY GOODNESS !

8. What is the voltage across a 100-ohm circuit element that draws a current of 1 A?

   _____

9. What voltage will produce 3 A through a 15-ohm resistor?

   _____

10. The current in an incandescent lamp is 0.5 A when connected to a 120-V circuit, and 0.2 A when connected to a 10-V source. Does the resistance of the lamp change in these cases? Explain your answer and defend it with numerical values.

    _____

    _____

Conceptual **PHYSICS**

Concept-Development Practice Page **34-2**

Electric Power

Recall that the rate energy is converted from one form to another is *power*.

$$\text{power} = \frac{\text{energy converted}}{\text{time}} = \frac{\text{voltage} \times \text{charge}}{\text{time}} = \text{voltage} \times \frac{\text{charge}}{\text{time}} = \text{voltage} \times \text{current}$$

The unit of power is the *watt* (or *kilowatt*). So in units form,

Electric power (*watts*) = current (*amperes*) x voltage (*volts*),

where 1 *watt = 1 ampere x 1 volt*.

THAT'S RIGHT··· VOLTAGE = $\frac{\text{ENERGY}}{\text{CHARGE}}$, SO ENERGY = VOLTAGE × CHARGE···
AND $\frac{\text{CHARGE}}{\text{TIME}}$ = CURRENT ⸘ NEAT ⸚

A 100-WATT BULB CONVERTS ELECTRIC ENERGY INTO HEAT AND LIGHT MORE QUICKLY THAN A 25-WATT BULB. THAT'S WHY FOR THE SAME VOLTAGE A 100-WATT BULB GLOWS BRIGHTER THAN A 25-WATT BULB!

1. What is the power when a voltage of 120 V drives a 2-A current through a device?

   _____

2. What is the current when a 60-W lamp is connected to 120 V?

   _____

WHICH DRAWS MORE CURRENT··· THE 100-WATT OR THE 25-WATT BULB?

3. How much current does a 100-W lamp draw when connected to 120 V?

   _____

4. If part of an electric circuit dissipates energy at 6 W when it draws a current of 3 A, what voltage is impressed across it?

   _____

5. The equation

   $$\text{power} = \frac{\text{energy converted}}{\text{time}}$$

   rearranged gives

   energy converted = _____

WATT'S HAPPENING?

6. Explain the difference between a kilowatt and a kilowatt-hour.

   _____

7. One deterrent to burglary is to leave your front porch light on all the time. If your fixture contains a 60-W bulb at 120 V, and your local power utility sells energy at 8 cents per kilowatt-hour, how much will it cost to leave the bulb on for the whole month? Show your work on the other side of this page.

Conceptual **PHYSICS**

Series Circuits

1. In the circuit shown at the right, a voltage of 6 V pushes charge through a single resistor of 2 Ω. According to Ohm's law, the current in the resistor (and therefore in the whole circuit) is

    _____ A.

2 Ω

6 V

THE EQUIVALENT RESISTANCE OF RESISTORS IN SERIES IS SIMPLY THEIR SUM!

2.

If a second identical lamp is added, as on the left, the 6-V battery must push charge through a total resistance of _____ Ω. The current in the circuit is then ____ A.

3 Ω

3 Ω

6 V

3. The equivalent resistance of three 4-Ω resistors in series is _____ Ω.

4. Does current flow *through* a resistor, or *across* a resistor? _____

    Is voltage established *through* a resistor, or *across* a resistor? _____

5. Does current in the lamps occur simultaneously, or does charge flow first through one lamp, then the other, and finally the last in turn?

    _____

6. Circuits *a* and *b* below are identical with all bulbs rated at equal wattage (therefore equal resistance). The only difference between the circuits is that Bulb 5 has a short circuit, as shown.

1   2   3

a   4.5 V

4   5   6

b   4.5 V

   a. In which circuit is the current greater? _____

   b. In which circuit are all three bulbs equally bright? _____

   c. What bulbs are the brightest? _____

   d. What bulb is the dimmest? _____

   e. What bulbs have the largest voltage drops across them? _____

   f. Which circuit dissipates more power? _____

   g. What circuit produces more light? _____

Conceptual PHYSICS

Parallel Circuits

THE SUM OF THE CURRENTS IN THE TWO BRANCH PATHS EQUALS THE CURRENT BEFORE IT DIVIDES.

1. In the circuit shown below, there is a voltage drop of 6 V across *each* 2-Ω resistor.

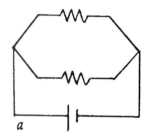

a. By Ohm's law, the current in *each* resistor is _____ A.

b. The current through the battery is the sum of the currents in the resistors, _____ A.

c. Fill in the current in the eight blank spaces in the view of the *same circuit* shown again at the right.

2. Cross out the circuit below that is *not* equivalent to the circuit above.

a

b

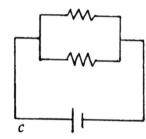

c

d

3. Consider the parallel circuit at the right.
   a. The voltage drop across each resistor is _____ V.

   b. The current in each branch is:
   2-Ω resistor _____A
   2-Ω resistor _____A
   1-Ω resistor _____A

   b. The current through the battery equals the sum of the currents which equals _____ A.

   c. The equivalent resistance of the circuit equals _____ Ω.

THE EQUIVALENT RESISTANCE OF A PAIR OF RESISTORS IN PARALLEL IS THEIR PRODUCT DIVIDED BY THEIR SUM!

Conceptual **PHYSICS**

Concept-Development Practice Page   **35-2**

Compound Circuits

1. The initial circuit, below left, is a compound circuit made of a combination of resistors. It is reduced to a single equivalent resistance by the three steps, the circuits to its right, *a*, *b*, *c.* In step *a*, show the equivalent resistance of the parallel 4-Ω resistors. In step *b* combine this in series with the 3-Ω resistor. In step *c*, combine the last parallel pair to obtain the equivalent resistance of the circuit. (Note the similarity of this circuit and Figure 35.10 in your textbook.)

Initial Circuit   *a.*   *b.*   *c.*

R = _____

2. The circuit below is similar to Figure 35.11 in your textbook. In three successive steps, as in Question 1, replace each pair of resistors by a single resistor of equivalent resistance.

R = _____

3. Find the equivalent resistance of these three circuits.

a   *b*

R = _____   R = _____

c

R = _____

Conceptual PHYSICS

4. The table beside circuit *a* below shows the current through each resistor, the voltage across each resistor, and the power dissipated as heat in each resistor. Find the similar correct values for circuits *b*, *c*, and *d*, and put your answers in the tables shown.

a 12 V

RESISTANCE	CURRENT ×	VOLTAGE =	POWER
2 Ω	2 A	4 V	8 W
4 Ω	2 A	8 V	16 W
6 Ω	2 A	12 V	24 W

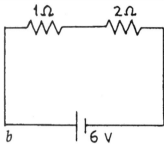

b 6 V

RESISTANCE	CURRENT ×	VOLTAGE =	POWER
1 Ω			
2 Ω			

c 6 V

RESISTANCE	CURRENT ×	VOLTAGE =	POWER
6 Ω			
3 Ω			

d 6 V

RESISTANCE	CURRENT ×	VOLTAGE =	POWER
2 Ω			
2 Ω			
1 Ω			

Magnetism

Fill in each blank with the appropriate word.

1. Attraction or repulsion of charges depends on their *signs,* positives or negatives. Attraction or repulsion of magnets depends on their magnetic _____:
    _____ or _____.

    YOU HAVE A MAGNETIC
    PERSONALITY !

2. Opposite poles attract; like poles _____.

3. A magnetic field is produced by the _____ of electric charge.

4. Clusters of magnetically aligned atoms are magnetic_____.

5. A magnetic _____ surrounds a current-carrying wire.

6. When a current-carrying wire is made to form a coil around a piece of iron, the result is an
    _____

7. A charged particle moving in a magnetic field experiences a deflecting _____ that is maximum when the charge moves
    _____ to the field.

8. A current-carrying wire experiences a deflecting
    _____that is maximum when the

    wire and magnetic field are _____ to one another.

9. A simple instrument designed to detect electric current is the_____ ;
    when calibrated to measure current, it is an _____ ; when calibrated to
    measure voltage, it is a _____.

    THEN TO REALLY MAKE
    THINGS "SIMPLE," THERE'S
    THE RIGHT-HAND RULE !

10. The largest size magnet in the world is the _____ itself.

Conceptual **PHYSICS**

11. The illllustration below is similar to Figure 36.4 in your textbook. Iron filings trace out patterns of magnetic field lines about a bar magnet. In the field are some magnetic compasses. The compass needle in only one compass is shown. Draw in the needles with proper orientation in the other compasses.

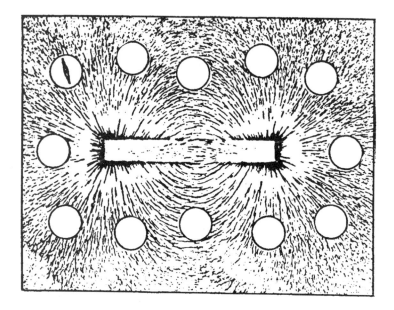

12. The illustration below is similar to Figure 36.13 (center) in your textbook. Iron filings trace out the magnetic field pattern about the loop of current-carrying wire. Draw in the compass needle orientations for all the compasses.

Faraday's Law

1. Hans Christian Oersted discovered that magnetism and electricity are

    (related)   (independent of each other).

    Magnetism is produced by

    (batteries)   (the motion of electric charges).

Faraday and Henry discovered that electric current can be produced by

    (batteries)   (motion of a magnet).

More specifically, voltage is induced in a loop of wire if there is a change in the

    (batteries)   (magnetic field in the loop).

This phenomenon is called

    (electromagnetism)   (electromagnetic induction).

2. When a magnet is plunged in and out of a coil of wire, voltage is induced in the coil. If the rate of the in-and-out motion of the magnet is doubled, the induced voltage

    (doubles)   (halves)   (remains the same).

    If instead the number of loops in the coil is doubled, the induced voltage

    (doubles)   (halves)   (remains the same).

3. A rapidly changing magnetic field in any region of space induces a rapidly changing

    (electric field)   (magnetic field)   (gravitational field)

    which in turn induces a rapidly changing

    (magnetic field)   (electric field)   (baseball field).

    This generation and regeneration of electric and magnetic fields makes up

    (electromagnetic waves)   (sound waves)   (both of these).

Conceptual **PHYSICS**

Transformers

Consider a simple transformer that has a 100-turn primary coil and a 1000-turn secondary coil. The primary is connected to a 120-V AC source and the secondary is connected to an electrical device with a resistance of 1000 ohms.

1. What will be the voltage output of the secondary?
   _____ V

2. What current flows in the secondary circuit? _____ A

3. Now that you know the voltage and the current, what is the power in the secondary coil? _____ W

4. Neglecting small heating losses, and knowing that energy is conserved, what is the power in the primary coil? _____ W

5. Now that you know the power and the voltage across the primary coil, what is the current drawn by the primary coil? _____ A

Circle the correct answers:

6. The results show voltage is stepped (up) (down) from primary to secondary, and that current is correspondingly stepped (up) (down).

7. For a step-up transformer, there are (more) (fewer) turns in the secondary coil than the primary: For such a transformer, there is (more) (less) current in the secondary than in the primary.

8. A transformer can step up (voltage) (energy and power), but in no way can it step up (voltage) (energy and power).

9. If 120 V is used to power a toy electric train that operates on 6 V, then a (step up) (step down) transformer should be used that has a primary to secondary turns ratio of (1/20) (20/1).

10. A transformer operates on (dc) (ac) because the magnetic field within the iron core must (continually change) (remain steady).

Conceptual **PHYSICS**

Power Transmission

6 000 V   120 000 V   2400 V   120 V

Many power companies provide power to cities that are far from the generators. Consider a city of 100 000 persons who each use continually use 120 W of power (equivalent to the operation of two 60-W light bulbs per person). The power constantly consumed is
100 000 persons x 120 W / person = 12 million W (12 MW).

1. What current corresponds to this amount of power at the common 120 V used by consumers?

$$P = IV$$
$$12\ 000\ 000\ W = I \times 120\ V$$

$$I = \frac{\qquad\qquad W}{V} = \qquad A$$

PHYSICS
SIGH

This is an enormous current, more than can be carried in the thickest of wires without overheating. More power would be dissipated in the form of heat than would reach the faraway city. Fortunately the important quantity is *IV* and not *I* alone. Power companies transmit power over long distances at very high voltages so that the current in the wires is low and heating of the power lines is minimized.

2. If the 12 MW of power is transmitted at 120 000 V, the current in the wires is

$$I = \frac{P}{V} = \frac{\qquad\qquad W}{V} = \qquad A$$

This amount of current can be carried in long-distance power lines with only small power losses due to heating (normally less than 1%). But the corresponding high voltages wired to houses would be very dangerous. So step-down transformers are used in the city.

3. What ratio of primary turns to secondary turns should be on a transformer to step 120 000 V down to 2400 V? _____

4. What ratio of primary turns to secondary turns should be on a transformer to step 2400 V down to 120 V used in household circuits? _____

5. What is the main benefit of ac compared to dc power?
_____

Conceptual **PHYSICS**

Chapter 37   Electromagnetic Induction

Power Production

Does it take a lot of water to light a light bulb? That depends on its wattage and how long it glows. In this practice page, you are to calculate the mass and volume of water that falls over a 10-m high dam to keep a 100-W light bulb glowing for 1 year.

USE YOUR CALCULATOR WITH THIS ONE?

1. First, calculate how many joules are required to keep the bulb lit for 1 year.

$$\text{Energy} = \text{power} \times \text{time} = 100\,\cancel{W} \times 1\,\cancel{yr} \times \frac{1\ J/\cancel{s}}{1\,\cancel{W}} \times \frac{365\,\cancel{d}}{1\,\cancel{yr}} \times \frac{24\,\cancel{h}}{1\,\cancel{d}} \times \frac{3600\,\cancel{s}}{1\,\cancel{h}}$$

$$= \underline{\hspace{3cm}}\ J$$

2. What mass of water elevated 10 m has this much PE? From Chapter 8, recall that gravitational PE = *mgh*:

$$PE = mgh$$

$$m = \frac{PE}{gh} = \frac{\underline{\hspace{3cm}}\ J}{(9.8\ m/s^2)(10\ m)} = \underline{\hspace{3cm}}\ kg$$

3. But this assumes 100% efficiency. A hydroelectric plant is typically 20% efficient. This means only 1 part in 5 of the PE of the falling water ends up as electricity. So the mass above must be multiplied by 5 to get the actual amount of water that must fall to keep the 100-W bulb lit.

$$5 \times \underline{\hspace{4cm}}\ kg = \underline{\hspace{4cm}}\ kg$$

4. This is an impressive number of kilograms! To visualize this amount of water, convert it to cubic meters. (Recall 1 kg of water occupies 1 liter, and there are 1000 liters in 1 cubic meter.)

$$\text{Volume} = \underline{\hspace{3cm}}\,\cancel{kg} \times 1\ \frac{\cancel{L}}{\cancel{kg}} \times \frac{1\ m^3}{1000\,\cancel{L}} = \underline{\hspace{3cm}}\ m^3$$

5. For comparison, an Olympic-size swimming pool holds about 4000 m³ of water. How many such poolfuls of water are required to keep a 100-W bulb lit for one year?

$$\text{Number of poolfuls} = \frac{\underline{\hspace{2cm}}\ m^3}{\underline{\hspace{1cm}}\ m^3/\text{poolful}} \approx \underline{\hspace{2cm}}\ \text{poolfuls}$$

Does it take a lot of water to light a light bulb? To light a city full of light bulbs? Now you have a better idea!

Conceptual PHYSICS

**Concept-Development
Practice Page** **38-1**

The Atom and the Quantum

1. To say that light is quantized means that light is made up of

    (elemental units)   (waves)

2. Compared to photons of low-frequency light, photons of higher-frequency light have more

    (energy)   (speed)   (quanta)

3. The photoelectric effect supports the

    (wave model of light)   (particle model of light)

4. The photoelectric effect is evident when light shone on certain photosensitive materials ejects

    (photons)   (electrons)

5. The photoelectric effect is more effective with violet light than with red light because the photons of violet light

    (resonate with the atoms in the material)

    (deliver more energy to the material)

    (are more numerous)

6. According to De Broglie's wave model of matter, a beam of light and a beam of electrons

    (are fundamentally different)   (are similar)

7. According to De Broglie, the greater the speed of an electron beam, the

    (greater is its wavelength)   (shorter is its wavelength)

8. The discreteness of the energy levels of electrons about the atomic nucleus is best understood by considering the electron to be a

    (wave)   (particle)

9. Heavier atoms are not appreciably larger in size than lighter atoms. The main reason for this is the greater nuclear charge

    (pulls surrounding electrons into tighter orbits)

    (holds more electrons about the atomic nucleus)   (produces a denser atomic structure)

10. Whereas in the everyday macroworld the study of motion is called *mechanics,* in the microworld the study of quanta is called

    (Newtonian mechanics)   (quantum mechanics)

Conceptual **PHYSICS**

A QUANTUM MECHANIC!

The Atomic Nucleus and Radioactivity

1. *Complete the following statements.*

   a. A lone neutron spontaneously decays into a proton plus an

   _____ .

   PHYSICS ≡SIGH≡

   b. Alpha and beta rays are made of streams of particles, whereas gamma rays are streams of _____ .

   c. An electrically charged atom is called an_____.

   d. Different _____ of an element are chemically identical but differ in the number of neutrons in the nucleus.

   e. Transuranic elements are those beyond atomic number_____.

   f. If the amount of a certain radioactive sample decreases by half in four weeks, in four more weeks the amount remaining should be _____ the original amount.

   g. Water from a natural hot spring is warmed by_____inside the earth.

2. The gas in the little girl's balloon is made up of former alpha and beta particles produced by radioactive decay.

   a. If the mixture is electrically neutral, how many more beta particles than alpha particles are in the balloon?

   _____

   _____

   b. Why is your answer not "same"?

   _____

   _____

   c. Why are the alpha and beta particles no longer harmful to the child?

   _____

   _____

   d. What element does this mixture make?

   _____

Conceptual **PHYSICS**

Radioactive Half Life

You and your classmates will now play the "half-life game." Each of you should have a coin to shake inside cupped hands. After it has been shaken for a few seconds, the coin is tossed on the table or on the floor. Students with tails up fall out of the game. Only those who consistently show heads remain in the game. Finally everybody has tossed a tail and the game is over.

1. On the graph below, plot the number of students left in the game after each toss. Draw a smooth curve that passes close to the points on your plot. What is the similarity of your curve with that shown in Figure 39.13 of your textbook?

   _____

   _____

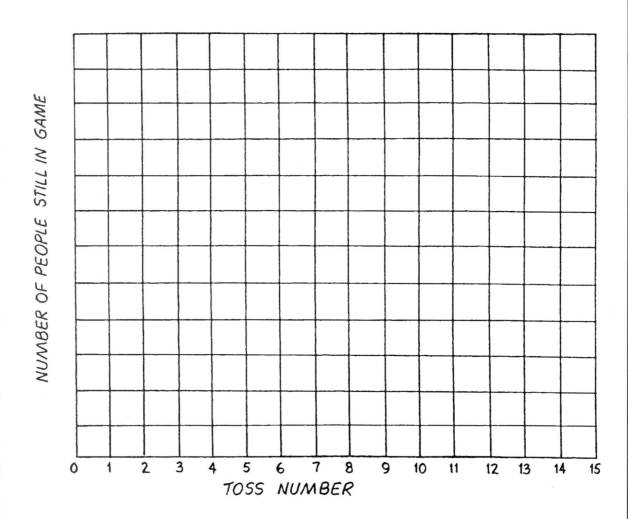

2. Was the person to last longest in the game *lucky*, with some sort of special powers to guide the long survival? What test could you make to decide the answer to this question?

   _____

   _____

Conceptual PHYSICS

Natural Transmutation

Fill in the decay-scheme diagram below, similar to that shown on page 619 in the textbook, but beginning with U-235 and ending up with an isotope of lead. Use the table at the left, and identify each element in the series with its chemical symbol.

Step	Particle emitted
1	Alpha
2	Beta
3	Alpha
4	Alpha
5	Beta
6	Alpha
7	Alpha
8	Alpha
9	Beta
10	Alpha
11	Beta
12	Stable

MASS NUMBER

235
231
227
223
219
215
211
207
203

81 82 83 84 85 86 87 88 89 90 91 92

ATOMIC NUMBER

What isotope is the final product? _____

Conceptual PHYSICS

Nuclear Reactions

Complete these nuclear reactions.

1. $^{238}_{92}\text{U} \rightarrow \,^{234}_{90}\text{Th} + \,^{4}_{2}\underline{\qquad}$

2. $^{234}_{90}\text{Th} \rightarrow \,^{234}_{91}\text{Pa} + \,^{0}_{-1}\underline{\qquad}$

3. $^{234}_{91}\text{Pa} \rightarrow \underline{\qquad} + \,^{4}_{2}\text{He}$

4. $^{220}_{86}\text{Rn} \rightarrow \underline{\qquad} + \,^{4}_{2}\text{He}$

5. $^{216}_{84}\text{Po} \rightarrow \underline{\qquad} + \,^{0}_{-1}\text{e}$

6. $^{216}_{84}\text{Po} \rightarrow \underline{\qquad} + \,^{4}_{2}\text{He}$

7. $^{210}_{83}\text{Bi} \rightarrow \underline{\qquad} + \,^{0}_{-1}\text{e}$

8. $^{1}_{0}\text{n} + \,^{10}_{5}\text{B} \rightarrow \underline{\qquad} + \,^{4}_{2}\text{He}$

Concept-Development Practice Page   **40-1**

Nuclear Fission and Fusion

1. Complete the table for a chain reaction in which two neutrons from each step individually cause a new reaction.

EVENT	1	2	3	4	5	6	7
NO. OF REACTIONS	1	2	4				

2. Complete the table for a chain reaction where three neutrons from each reaction cause a new reaction.

EVENT	1	2	3	4	5	6	7
NO. OF REACTIONS	1	3	9				

3. Complete these beta reactions, which occur in a breeder reactor.

$$^{239}_{92}U \rightarrow \underline{\hspace{1.5cm}} + ^{0}_{-1}e$$

$$^{239}_{93}Np \rightarrow \underline{\hspace{1.5cm}} + ^{0}_{-1}e$$

4. Complete the following fission reactions.

$$^{1}_{0}n + ^{235}_{92}U \rightarrow ^{143}_{54}Xe + ^{90}_{38}Sr + \underline{\hspace{0.5cm}}(^{1}_{0}n)$$

$$^{1}_{0}n + ^{235}_{92}U \rightarrow ^{152}_{60}Nd + \underline{\hspace{1cm}} + 4(^{1}_{0}n)$$

$$^{1}_{0}n + ^{239}_{94}Pu \rightarrow \underline{\hspace{1cm}} + ^{97}_{40}Zr + 2(^{1}_{0}n)$$

5. Complete the following fusion reactions.

$$^{2}_{1}H + ^{2}_{1}H \rightarrow ^{3}_{2}He + \underline{\hspace{1cm}}$$

$$^{2}_{1}H + ^{3}_{1}H \rightarrow ^{4}_{2}He + \underline{\hspace{1cm}}$$

KNOW NUKES!

Conceptual PHYSICS

